BREAKING
CONTROLLING
POWERS

Learning How to Protect
Your Spirit, Soul, and Body

by

Roberts Liardon

ALBURY PUBLISHING
Tulsa, Oklahoma

Breaking Controlling Powers
Learning How to Protect Your Spirit, Soul, and Body
ISBN 1-57778-089-2
Copyright © 1998 by Roberts Liardon Ministries
P. O. Box 30710
Laguna Hills, California 92654

Published by ALBURY PUBLISHING
P. O. Box 470406
Tulsa, Oklahoma 74147-0406

CONTENTS

INTRODUCTION

The purpose of this book is to alert us to the different strategies that Satan uses to exert his control over us so that we can get free and stay free. In the past, we have been too vague in the area of spiritual warfare. Most believers know they are under attack, but they cannot describe it or even understand why or how they came to be in a difficult situation.

The truth is, even as believers we can have some degree of demonic control operating in our lives, and this prevents us from living the abundant life that Jesus promised in John 10:10. That is why it is important that we learn to accurately discern where we are being controlled and why. If we can understand this, we will know how to effectively fight and recover.

Controlling powers manifest in different forms. Maybe you are under the abusive control of another individual. If that is the case, both you and your controller are miserable. Why not get things right with God? Why not learn to break the power of the controlling spirit and all the spirits that go with it — fear, guilt, obligation, confusion, and frustration?

Or maybe you have an area of sin in your life that seems impossible to break. Every time you make a New Year's resolution to get rid of it, you find yourself falling to your flesh within days.

We can say *no* to the enemy. We can say *no* to our desires, to the flesh, to this world, to people, to our circumstances, and to the devil! And we can say *yes* to God and all that He has for us — peace, comfort, freedom, and victory. That's what this book is all about.

James 4:7 says, **Submit yourselves therefore to God. Resist the devil, and he will flee from you.** When we stay focused on God — listening to and then obeying His Spirit and His Word — we can recognize the enemy's evil strategies in our lives and stop him in his tracks. Then God's blessings can flow freely and we will live the abundant life He desires for us to live.

It's time to break any controlling power in your life that's not Jesus Christ!

CHAPTER 1

WHO IS OUR ENEMY?

I had just returned from an exhausting schedule of ministry. The meetings had been good and lives were changed. I was happy and at peace. When I retired for the evening, I was totally relaxed knowing everything was calm and in order.

But things were about to change.

At three o'clock in the morning, the shrill ringing of my telephone pierced the night and abruptly ended my blissful rest. I fumbled the telephone receiver to my ear and from the other end a frantic voice whined, "Roberts! Roberts! Help me...help me."

After listening to the circumstances my distraught friend found himself in, I interrupted and said, "You are not seeing clearly. This is not a problem — it's the devil."

"The devil!?" He was shocked.

"That's right. It's the devil. You are being attacked and don't even know it."

As I continued to talk to him into the wee hours of the morning, I began to realize that many Christians do not know the tactics of their enemy. They may be good, faithful people, filled with the love and zeal of God, and still be totally ignorant when it comes to the schemes of the devil.

KNOW HIS TACTICS

Lest Satan should get an advantage of us: for we are not ignorant of his devices.

2 Corinthians 2:11

We have a mandate, a commission from God, to know our enemy. If we as believers do not understand or comprehend Satan's tactics, then he will get an advantage over us. If we do not know the way our enemy operates, then he will deceive us and possibly destroy us.

Believers should not be afraid to discuss the devil. Jesus mentioned and taught about him very often in the New Testament. Jesus did not *exalt* the devil by discussing him — He *exposed* him. He taught the truth about God and exposed the lies the enemy had perpetrated against Him. He also dealt openly with Satan and his demons and taught the people their authority over him.

Exposing the devil is not our priority — *knowing* God is. But anything that hinders our relationship with God or attempts to abort His plan in the earth must be properly understood and dealt with.

We have been purchased and bought by the blood of Jesus. This entitles us to the benefits of the finished works of Christ, but the new birth does not automatically eliminate demonic influence or demonic attack. Even Jesus personally dealt with Satan in the wilderness and throughout His public ministry.

The disciples also had to stand against the wiles of the devil in their own lives. Peter attempted to persuade Jesus not to go to the cross in Matthew 16:20-22. Although he vowed undying loyalty, Jesus told him he would deny Him three times, which he did. (See Matthew 26:33,34,74.) Demonic power influenced Judas to betray Jesus. (See Matthew 26:21-25.) When James and John did not like the actions of the Samaritans, Jesus rebuked them and told them, **"Ye know not what manner of spirit ye are of"** (Luke 9:55). Demonic influence and attack will come and attempt to persuade us to err or to sin no matter what level of maturity we walk in.

DO NOT BE IGNORANT

My people are destroyed for lack of knowledge.

Hosea 4:6

Lack of knowledge in the area of demonic influence has caused many believers to fall. Many open the doors of calamity, destruction, and even death by not knowing the intention of their enemy.

When Jesus gave us the Great Commission before He left the earth, He said, **In my name shall they cast out devils** (Mark 16:17). We cannot cast out something we do not recognize or understand.

Ignorance immobilizes us, causing us to remain passive in an area where we lack understanding. Ignorance gives ground and entrance to the schemes of the devil. Ignorance works for the enemy because it gives him freedom to pursue and conquer without being noticed.

When we do not properly discern the schemes of the enemy, our families, our churches, our nation, and every other sphere of our lives are negatively affected. We must preach and know the whole Gospel, not just a part of it. When we refuse to recognize our enemy, we become prey to him. When we shrink away from truth and refuse to examine it or learn from it, we remain unprepared for the attacks of a raging enemy.

The Bible is not ashamed to discuss and expose the devil. From Genesis to Revelation, the entire plan and purpose of our enemy unfolds. It is our responsibility to train and mature ourselves through prayer, the Word, the leading of the Holy Spirit, and the authority God has positioned over us.

Because some believers fail to take the responsibility of maturing themselves, the plan of God is thwarted in their lives. As a result, they try to live in the midst of an attack and do not understand why they act the way they do or think the way they think. They write it off as their personality or their circumstances.

I am not saying that every negative situation we face is a demon. Many times we find ourselves in trouble because of undisciplined flesh and desires. But even a Christian who does not discipline their flesh has opened the door to the enemy, which compounds the problem.

The Word of God was written for our instruction — to teach and train us. Written on the pages of the Bible are truths of life, health, and peace. If we fall, through those truths we can stand again. By embracing those truths, we are healed if sickness comes. As we mature our spirit man through prayer and the Word, we don't have to fall prey to deception. We can effectively stand, conquer, and prevail when an attack comes by embracing the Word of God as our safeguard.

TYPES OF CONTROL

There is a great struggle going on in the world today between the forces of light (Christianity) and the forces of darkness (satanic powers). We must realize that what happens in the spiritual realm is reflected in the natural realm. In other words, what you choose to allow to control you spiritually determines what manifests in the natural.

There are basically three types of control. There is a natural control that people exert over others, a *self-control* that must be exercised within the individual, and an *abusive control* that is exercised by one person over another. Some means of control are more obvious than others, but if Satan can control a person, that person will be held in unnecessary bondage and hindered from fulfilling the purpose of God in their life.

We must understand these three types of control to accurately discern their influences. Parents exert a *natural* control over their small children as part of training them in the way they should go. (See Proverbs 22:6.) Teachers must maintain control in the classroom in order to create a conducive learning environment. To some degree, employers exert control over their employees to insure productivity for the company and the employees.

Exercising *self-control* by applying the Word of God to our lives and obeying the voice of the Holy Spirit keep us free from sin. Self-control keeps us from harming ourselves and others. When we refuse to insult someone who has just offended us and choose to pray for them instead, peace reigns in our lives. When we cast down vain imaginations about someone else's spouse, our own marriage grows stronger and the enemy cannot gain entrance to it.

Natural control and self-control are godly traits, but the third type of control can destroy us, and that is *abusive control*. Abusive control can be defined as an attempt to dominate another person in order to fulfill one's own desires and to enhance personal security. This type of control is demonic. Although the controller may appear to handle everything with ease and confidence, in reality they are in bondage to demons — scared, intimidated, insecure, and unfulfilled. They are terribly afraid of being rejected. Manipulation of others is a means for them to feel superior and secure. The controller's goal is survival at any cost.

People who exercise abusive control seek to become the deciding factor in the lives of others. Such individuals replace the Word of God as the balance in the lives of those they dominate. They react negatively if they do not have control of all decisions made. There is no personal regard or consideration for the one being controlled and dominated.

Although Communism has deteriorated, many people have and still do suffer enormously as a result of the ungodly control exercised by Communist regimes. Such totalitarian governments dominate people through fear, ignorance, and poverty, restricting their knowledge of the outside world and limiting their freedom of expression and religion.

However, people living in free societies are not immune to abusive control. This control may come from parents, spouses, family members, friends, creditors, co-workers, spiritual leaders, and even children. Christians must recognize the core problem of abusive control and understand its negative actions and reactions. Then they can be set free and effectively minister to those who are still in bondage.

HOW ABUSIVE CONTROL TAKES OVER

Abusive control does not originate in strangers. The devil does not use the beggar on the street to control the life of a Christian or the body of Christ.

If a stranger walked into your home or down the aisle of your church, announcing that he had come on the premises to take over, you would throw him out. But if someone you knew and trusted were to come on the scene for the same purpose, you would not be so quick to eject him.

At some point in the future, someone you respect right now may decide not to go on following the Lord. If you are not secure in the Lord yourself, this situation could cause a great problem in your life, your destiny, and your church. You must find your source of being in God and be able to discern accurately in the spirit to recognize the controlling attacks of the enemy.

When we place our security in something or someone other than God, we open ourselves to deception, despair, and defeat. It is true that we need others to help encourage and sharpen us, but our dependency should be upon God, not people. We should never base our lives on the opinions of others. We should compare *people's words* with *God's words*, and follow the leading and direction of the Holy Spirit.

HOW TO RECOGNIZE AN ABUSIVE CONTROLLER

An abusive controller is *obsessed with supervising the behavior of others.* Their entire focus is on someone or something other than themselves. They cannot define the direction or describe the plan for their own life, because they are so wrapped up in the person they are controlling.

An abusive controller *stifles the creative move of the Spirit through the person under his power.* Because they are bound by fear and thus control others by fear, they hinder the ability of others to be themselves. Many abusive controllers have a genuine desire to see the move of

God operate accurately and successfully, but in attempting to promote that move, they can become religious and smother the true call and gifts of those around them.

An abusive controller has a *selfish personality*. They make demands easily, and often these demands are ruthless.

An abusive controller has a *low sense of self-worth*. They usually avoid open expressions of feelings or direct honest communication. Instead of dealing with their own problem, they turn their entire focus on the problems of others. Fed by their sense of personal rejection, they base their life and the result of it on what they can accomplish through their own works. They look at those around them as their own accomplishments. If others fail, they feel they are a failure also. If those they control are rejected, they feel rejected. This sense of rejection is clearly demonic. Whether we are accepted or rejected by others has nothing to do with our value or worth as children of God. Whenever our security lies in something or someone other than God, it will fail.

We must understand that abusive control is an *illusion* — an imaginary sense of power used by the devil to deceive the one who wields it — and the enemy is a pro at deception! No one can control the life and emotions of another. God gave mankind a free will, and He will not violate our gift of choice and decision. We can only change and control our own self. The Holy Spirit does not use illusion or fantasy in dealing with people's hearts.

Abusive control is undermining and secretive. It is accompanied by an unnatural attachment, and every relationship it touches crumbles in destruction.

Manipulation is the main tool of the abusive controller to keep others in bondage to him. Jesus managed to remove Himself from people who sought to abusively control Him.

ABUSIVE CONTROL IN RELIGION
And when the devil had ended all the temptation, he

departed from him for a season.

And Jesus returned in the power of the Spirit into Galilee: and there went out a fame of him through all the region round about.

And he taught in their synagogues, being glorified of all.

And he came to Nazareth, where he had been brought up: and, as his custom was, he went into the synagogue on the sabbath day, and stood up for to read.

And there was delivered unto him the book of the prophet Esaias. And when he had opened the book, he found the place where it was written,

The Spirit of the Lord is upon me, because he hath anointed me to preach the gospel to the poor; he hath sent me to heal the brokenhearted, to preach deliverance to the captives, and recovering of sight to the blind, to set at liberty them that are bruised.

To preach the acceptable year of the Lord.

And he closed the book, and he gave it again to the minister, and sat down. And the eyes of all them that were in the synagogue were fastened on him.

And he began to say unto them, This day is this scripture fulfilled in your ears.

Luke 4:13-21

When the rabbi handed the scrolls to Jesus, He opened them and read Isaiah 61:1,2. But Jesus did not read this prophecy as a normal man would read it. Jesus read the prophetic message as if it applied to Him — because it did! The people of Nazareth totally missed the significance of Jesus' declaration that He was the Messiah. All they could say was, "No! You can't be the Messiah. You're the son of Joseph, the local carpenter." They became enraged at Jesus and intended to hurl Him down a cliff, but Jesus just walked right on through the crowd. Jesus knew His destiny. He knew His call to the earth. Even the ones whom Jesus loved most could not control Him or hinder what God had called Him to do. He wasn't going to be manipulated by Satan or by people, and neither should we.

The people of Nazareth were so astonished at Jesus that they did not simply glance at Him — their eyes were *fastened* on Him. After He had spoken strongly about their lack of faith in Him as the promised Messiah (Luke 4:23-27), their look became warlike — a look of madness, a look of rage, a look beyond natural understanding, a look that demands to know, "Who do you think you are?" When you take possession of what is yours spiritually, people who are lukewarm will automatically oppose you!

Has anyone ever looked at you that way? If you are a true servant of God, you may undergo this type of persecution.

Jesus did not respond to their anger, and because He didn't, they wanted to destroy Him! This was Jesus, the young man who had grown up in their "church." This was Nazareth, one of those small towns where everyone knows everyone else — and everyone supposedly loves everyone else.

The people of Nazareth wanted to kill Jesus because He did not withdraw, explain, or falter. He stood His ground. They could not control Him. He was not under their power. When you get to the place where people can't control you through intimidation or other means, they may try to destroy you.

After all the teachings He had delivered and all the miracles He had performed among them, they still did not believe that Jesus was the Messiah, because they had been blinded by *religion.*

Religion is an attempt to know and please God through *human* effort. Christianity is not a religion, it is a *relationship* with God — walking side by side, talking and communicating with Jesus, the living Son of God. This personal relationship does not come through religion, in which people seek to know and please God through human achievement and personal opinion.

Controlling spirits and religious spirits are like twins. It is hard to have one without the other. Religious spirits are demons sent to bind people from knowing the fullness of God. They are controlling spirits — hindering the true move of the Spirit of God. They use fleshly operations and manifestations to make people feel that they have done a service to God. They operate through those who walk by the flesh — those who do not know much about life in the Spirit. Such people are very unlearned about a spiritual relationship with Jesus Christ. However, they know all the "religious" facts, and usually distort them to control the move of the Holy Spirit.

THE EARLY CHURCH FACES RELIGIOUS CONTROL

The fourth chapter of Acts gives us an example of attempted control in the early church.

And as they spake unto the people, the priests, and the captain of the temple, and the Sadducees, came upon them,

Being grieved that they taught the people, and preached through Jesus the resurrection from the dead.

And they laid hands on them, and put them in hold unto the next day: for it was now eventide.

And it came to pass on the morrow, that their rulers, and elders, and scribes,

And Annas the high priest, and Caiaphas, and John, and Alexander, and as many as were of the kindred of the high priest, were gathered together at Jerusalem.

And when they had set them in the midst, they asked, By what power, or by what name, have ye done this?

Then Peter, filled with the Holy Ghost, said unto them, Ye rulers of the people, and elders of Israel,

If we this day be examined of the good deed done to the impotent man, by what means he is made whole;

Be it known unto you all, and to all the people of Israel,

that by the name of Jesus Christ of Nazareth, whom ye crucified, whom God raised from the dead, even by him doth this man stand here before you whole.

Acts 4:1-3,5-10

All the religious spirits in town had come together to attack Peter and John for healing a sick man! This tells us that religious spirits are not on the side of God, because no one should be angry when a sick person is healed. Instead, there should be rejoicing!

Have you noticed from this passage of Scripture that people who are "religious" have no common sense? Religious people think they are on fire for God, but in reality they are very cold spiritually. When someone tells them they are cold spiritually, or when God uses someone outside of their control system, they become very angry.

Peter was not afraid to respond to strong religious people. To effectively stand up to controlling, religious spirits, you must never fear them and always have a spiritual response ready. When abusive controllers began to attack God's servants in the Bible, their response was always one of righteousness. They spoke the truth with a boldness that came from the anointing of the Holy Spirit.

The religious leaders of Jerusalem were attacking the apostles to stop them from healing the people in the name of Jesus. The leaders were afraid that the healings would affect their control over the people. Peter, being full of the Holy Spirit, explained to all the religious leaders that healing people is a good deed, not a wicked or mischievous deed.

When confronting controlling people, state the truth, don't just suggest it. Peter told the leaders that the healing had come about **by the name of Jesus Christ of Nazareth, whom ye crucified** (Acts 4:10).

These same leaders had allowed a murderer to go free in order to have Jesus crucified, so Peter's bold statements didn't make these controlling, religious people very happy. They marveled at the apostles, but they were also very fearful of them.

Now when they saw the boldness of Peter and John, and perceived that they were unlearned and ignorant men, they marvelled; and they took knowledge of them, that they had been with Jesus.

And beholding the man which was healed standing with them, they could say nothing against it.

But when they had commanded them to go aside out of the council, they conferred among themselves,

Saying, What shall we do to these men? for that indeed a notable miracle hath been done by them is manifest to all them that dwell in Jerusalem; and we cannot deny it.

But that it spread no further among the people, let us straitly threaten them, that they speak henceforth to no man in this name.

And they called them, and commanded them not to speak at all nor teach in the name of Jesus.

Acts 4:13-18

Controllers don't ask, they command. If you are not standing on God's Word and walking in the Spirit, this demanding, threatening attitude will cause you to feel obligated to comply with their desires. You will go against what you believe, submitting to those who are intimidating you. That is abusive control, and you have allowed it!

Verse 17 states, ...**let us straitly threaten them....** A threat makes a person go against what they believe; it forces them to submit to those who are intimidating them.

The religious leaders of that day threatened the apostles by commanding **them not to speak at all nor teach in the name of Jesus.** That was control, and Peter and John had to decide how they would respond to it.

How did Peter and John react in the face of the threats and demands?

But Peter and John answered and said unto them,

Whether it be right in the sight of God to hearken unto you more than unto God, judge ye.

For we cannot but speak the things which we have seen and heard.

So when they had further threatened them, they let them go, finding nothing how they might punish them, because of the people: for all men glorified God for that which was done.

Acts 4:19-21

I like these apostles! They stood their ground before all the religious spirits in town. The religious leaders were angry both because a miracle had been done and it hadn't been done through them! They thought they should have been the ones to perform the miracle, because they were the religious rulers. However, because they were full of pride, God could not use them.

It often bothers some well-educated, proud people when God uses someone who has little or no formal education to be a miracle-worker. People filled with pride usually criticize those who have nothing in the natural. But how can God use those who are relying on their education alone? The only way an education works for a person is by submitting it to the will of God and not relying upon it, but upon God.

THE HOLY SPIRIT'S ROLE IN DEFEATING ABUSIVE CONTROL

God is not looking for a person who operates by his own way of thinking. God is looking for someone who operates from his heart. God is looking for those who will be obedient to the Holy Spirit.

And the spirit of the Lord shall rest upon him, the spirit of wisdom and understanding, the spirit of counsel and might, the spirit of knowledge and of the fear of the Lord.

Isaiah 11:2

The only way to defeat abusive control is to be full of the Holy Spirit. A special enduement of the Holy Spirit Peter operated in when the religious Jews attempted to control the early church was the spirit of might. Though it is important to speak words of faith and not of doubt, the spirit of might does not come upon a person as a result of reciting positive confessions or following prescribed formulas. It will not stay on an individual just because he associates with the "right people."

The spirit of might places a passion within the believer that motivates him to hate evil, and it will empower him to carry out God's plan. It is like a nuclear force resident within an individual, propelling him forward over every evil opponent that may attempt to restrain him.

The spirit of might confronts resistance. It provides the believer the ability to distinguish right from wrong in any situation and to act accordingly. It never defends; it simply endows us with the power to proclaim the truth and then do the right thing.

The spirit of might gives us a supernatural peace — one that passes all understanding — and a rest in the midst of battle. (See Philippians 4:7.) We can have assurance of the coming victory.

The spirit of might also endows the physical body and the emotions with endurance and protection. He supplies us with a supernatural ability to carry on far beyond our natural limitations.

The spirit of might never comes upon a person for the purpose of self-gain. It comes in order that the purpose of God may be fulfilled in the earth through the Church.

Peter had the spirit of might in and upon him as he spoke in the face of the religious leaders of his day. Peter said, "By the name of Jesus Christ of Nazareth — Whom you crucified — that's by Whose name we performed this miracle, and by Whose name we will continue to perform miracles!" (See Acts 4:10.)

The religious leaders responded by commanding the apostles to stop teaching and preaching in this name, threatening them severely if they did not obey. But, what did Peter and John do? They went back to their own company and told everyone of the things that had happened.

Did the Church in the book of Acts shrink back because of the report they received from the apostles? No! The spirit of might came on all of them! Instead of hiding in their homes and asking God to slay their enemies, they got down on their faces and asked the Lord to grant them more boldness. (See Acts 4:18-31.)

The Lord was so pleased with their response and request that the place where they were assembled was shaken, and they were all filled with the Holy Spirit. They became united with one heart and one purpose, and none of them lacked anything. Much to the horror of the religious, controlling leaders of that day, God gave great power to those who believed. (See Acts 4:31-34.) The result was that more healings, more deliverances, and more salvation experiences took place in the city of Jerusalem after Peter and John had been threatened than before!

Let this be our *testimony* today. Ask God to fill you with His power so you may blast through abusive, controlling spirits, then fulfill the plan and purpose of God in your life!

CHAPTER 2

DEALING WITH THE ENEMY

The United States has several different branches of the military that train and equip young men and women for battle. They undergo extensive drills to learn the strategy of their enemy. Not only do they develop an expertise with their weaponry, they also are taught to recognize the conditions for an attack and the situations that are conducive to one.

Those in the military are loyal and committed to protect what is theirs by boundary. They know the importance of unity in winning a battle. They are drilled in diligence and skill for the sake of their nation and loved ones.

Their intense training pays off when a surprise attack comes. The months they spent jumping up at the crack of dawn and the repeated examination of their weapons enable them to respond without much thought. The constant drill places a law inside of them; not a formula. They develop a bond with their weapons. They would not think of approaching enemy territory without them. An unarmed soldier would be a joke!

The weeks of crawling through a field on their chest with bullets flying overhead allows them to face obstacles without fear. They know where a land mine is most likely to be located. They can detect an approaching enemy. They know when to take cover and when to attack. They are trained and equipped. Their security comes from their preparation and insight.

Just as our military soldiers train for a conflict, we must train ourselves for spiritual conflict. The problem comes when we have not taken the time to train ourselves. We turn a "deaf ear" to the sound of the enemy, until one day we finally wake up and wonder why we are in the condition we're in! When the battle is over, it is easy to recognize that it was an attack of the enemy, but we should know before the battle ever starts that the adversary is out to destroy us.

GODLY CONFRONTATION

Godly confrontation results from a mature spirit man, seasoned by the Word of God and led by the Holy Spirit. The first time you felt an impression that something was not right, did you *ignore* it or *confront* it? Do you heed warning signs that trouble is near, or do you look away? We must learn to confront those things that stand between us and all that God has for us.

When we ignore a bad situation, it only worsens. Our marriage and home aren't destroyed overnight. Poverty does not suddenly overtake us. Uncontrolled desires will not simply disappear. The devil won't go away if you leave him an open door, and ignoring destructive situations will only cause the downfall of your family, your health, and eventually your life.

When we hear the word "confront," we often think of loud aggression. There are times that confrontation is loud. Sometimes a person has been led so far by the enemy, he must be "jerked" back into reality. But I'm talking about the confrontation that destroys the yoke of bondage. It may be a soft answer, a counteraction, or a loud confrontation, but they are all direct and productive when led by God. They are all works of boldness. Jesus was the meekest man on earth, but He was not weak. He never failed to confront the works of the devil. He spoke the truth, but His methods of presentation were according to each circumstance.

Confronting is good and it is godly. It has its place and we cannot be afraid of it. It is a part of the Gospel. Confronting must only come from the unction of the Spirit; not the emotion of a groomed personality.

NOT THE PERSON

For we wrestle not against flesh and blood, but against principalities, against powers, against the rulers of the darkness of this world, against spiritual wickedness in high places.

Ephesians 6:12

You must realize in your heart that you are not fighting a person. If you fall into the scheme that you are fighting a *natural* person or problem during a spiritual attack, you will revert to natural means. You will not win if you choose the road of gossip, slander, or revenge. *You cannot have soulish discussion to ease spiritual pressure.*

Spiritual warfare means there is a *spiritual influence* over someone or something. This demonic influence will hardly ever come through the same person or thing every time. As soon as you "catch on" to the fact that the devil is using someone or something to attack you, you can stop it by taking authority over it in Jesus' name. The attack can only continue if you are not committed to staying free and again fall under the influence of the people or things bringing oppression or evil into your life.

If the devil cannot defeat you through one person, he will wait awhile and try for one who is closer to you. He did the same with Jesus. The enemy attacked the ministry of Jesus through the multitudes and the religious leaders of the day. When Jesus remained unmoved, the devil tried for the disciples. But he only fully succeeded in conquering Judas. Even though the attack came through one closest to Him, Jesus knew the source and remained unhindered. He knew His mission, and He kept His eyes on it. Even on the cross, Jesus said:

Father, forgive them; for they know not what they do.

Luke 23:34

Forgiveness keeps you in the Spirit and causes you to win every time.

TEST THE SOURCE

Let no man say when he is tempted, I am tempted of God: for God cannot be tempted with evil, neither tempteth he any man.

James 1:13

We must know the character of God to recognize an attack. If we really know who God is and how He operates, we will be able to detect and destroy the devices of the enemy. For example, God does not redeem us from something, then test us with it. He doesn't put sickness, disease, death, or poverty on us to teach humility. Romans 8:28 tells us that **all things work together for good to them that love God,** but never will He *cause* you to go through something He paid for at the cross.

The enemy will whisper, "You are an unworthy soul."

You might say, "That's right."

Then he'll say, "God is going to teach you something through sickness and disease.

Again you respond, "That's right," and the next thing you know, we're burying you.

So many talk doubt and unbelief, giving glory to the enemy, while thinking they are being humble for God. If we have lessons to learn, we can learn them through prayer, the Word, and godly leadership. Why suffer under the hand of the enemy, blame God, and then — if we live through it — say we've "learned something"?

TEMPTATION AND WILES

The devil plans his attacks. He has a strategy for every situation. Satan will work his strategy either by *temptations* or *wiles*.

Temptations are obvious — outright blatant words, exposures, or situations. The enemy usually tempts us in an area that has caused trouble in the past, an area we have not dealt with. The temptation is designed for us to sin and to harden our heart against the Spirit of the Lord.

But every man is tempted, when he is drawn away of his own lust, and enticed.

Then when lust hath conceived, it bringeth forth sin: and sin, when it is finished, bringeth forth death.

James 1:14,15

Jesus Himself **was in all points tempted like as we are, yet without sin** (Hebrews 4:15). His identification with us and His death on the cross paid for our freedom from the clutches of sin. Those who trust in the Lord during times of temptation are safe and secure. Second Peter 2:9 says, **The Lord knoweth how to deliver the godly out of temptations.**

A wile is a scheme that is hidden to deceive and is not quite so obvious as a temptation. It intends to lure us as if by a magic spell, craftily covering itself to lead us into deception.

Put on the whole armour of God, that ye may be able to stand against the wiles of the devil.

Ephesians 6:11

Although the Bible uses the word "wiles" only once in the New Testament, Scripture repeatedly warns us of deceptions. Those who have embraced a wile are deceived when:

They are a hearer of the Word but not a doer. (See James 1:22.)

They think they have no sin. (See 1 John 1:8.)

They think they are something when they are nothing. (See Galatians 6:3.)

They think they are wise with the wisdom of the world. (See 1 Corinthians 3:18.)

They never miss church, yet they have an unbridled tongue. (See James 1:26)

They think they can sow unrighteousness, but not reap what they've sown. (See Galatians 6:7.)

They think the unrighteous can inherit the kingdom of God. (See 1 Corinthians 6:9.)

They think contact and communion with sin will not affect them. (See 1 Corinthians 15:33.)

They think they can get away with sin and lack repentance. (See 1 Timothy 4:1,2.)

Truth is the only antidote for deception. We can be alerted to every scheme if we will listen to the Holy Spirit within us. We may not understand it completely, but we are to judge everything by the Scriptures and by the character of God. Those two safeguards will ground an enemy missile every time.

DEMONIC RANK

We must learn to discern the level of our enemy. Like our military, the devil has rank, order, and governments in his kingdom. It is important that we know who they are.

For we wrestle not against flesh and blood, but against principalities, against powers, against the rulers of the darkness of this world, against spiritual wickedness in high places.

Ephesians 6:12

Every evil spirit has their assigned position. To recognize the level of attack, we must see their sphere of influence.

Principalities are the force and dominion that deal with nations and governments. The order of the government in a nation and the economy of the world can be influenced by principalities.

Powers have authority and power to take action in any sphere that is open to them. Wherever entrance is given that will affect a multitude, the work of an evil power will be searching for an opening.

Rulers of darkness are evil spirits that govern the darkness and blindness of the world, keeping people from seeing the wickedness and deception around them.

Wicked spirits operate from heavenly places through wiles and deceptions. Their target is the church. Fiery darts, onslaughts, doctrines of devils, and every false work are feats they are capable of planning.

There are also demons that are of a lower degree. These spirits are dumb. They scream, holler, harass, and aggravate. They have a little bit of power, but they can only bother us if we fear them.

The high ranking spirits are very smart. They watch what we say, where we look, and where we go. Then they go back with their information and plan a strategy against us. Their purpose is to destroy the body of Christ.

Great ministries have fallen because a high level attack was strategically implemented against them and not recognized until it was too late. We must learn the enemy's methods of attack in order to recognize them.

STAY HUNGRY!

The first sign that a person is under attack is that they lose their spiritual hunger for God. Just as physical appetite leaves a person who is sick in their body, spiritual hunger is the first thing to leave a person under spiritual attack. They are not hungry for the things of God. They don't want to go to church, they don't want to pray, and they don't want to read their Bible. God is no longer first in their lives.

Blessed are they which do hunger and thirst after righteousness: for they shall be filled.

Matthew 5:6

We must protect our spiritual hunger at all costs. If we do not hunger and thirst for the things of God, there will be no infilling of righteousness. As a result, we give entrance to the enemy, because an empty vessel will be filled with something — good or evil. Have you ever known a person who was really on fire for God and got "hit" by the enemy only to fade away? Did you ever see someone expressive and free in praise and worship suddenly turn still and cold? The enemy has quenched their hunger and desire for God, and they are in a very dangerous place. Spiritual hunger motivates us to go on with God, just as physical hunger motivates us to eat. Spiritual hunger is an acquired taste. It sustains life.

Even when you might not feel like reading the Bible, pick it up and read it anyway! The Bible is alive, even when we feel dead. The written Word of God is one of our weapons of warfare. Learn to use it to feed yourself and sustain the life inside of you. A marine may not always feel like pulling out his rifle, taking it apart, cleaning it, and putting it back together, but he knows that weapon will save his life in combat. The same is true for the Word of God. We may not always feel like taking it out, reading it, and letting it adjust and cleanse us, but it will be our shield and buckler in spiritual combat.

How do you become spiritually hungry? How do you stay spiritually hungry? It's simple. It's not always easy, but it's simple. You walk your bedroom floor and make yourself get hungry for God. You say out of your mouth, "I want more of You, God." Even when your mind says, "No you don't," you say, "Yes I do. Shut up."

You have to learn to talk to yourself and tell yourself how to think. That is how you take control of your mind and teach it to flow with the Word of God.

God cannot use someone who is divided within themselves. For example, your mind is thinking of cooking the evening meal the whole time you are praying, it is a divided prayer. A fervent prayer that produces results is from one whose mind agrees, whose flesh is subdued, and whose spirit leads them. You have got to be together, spirit, mind, and body. That kind of prayer will see results. That is the prayer of a righteous man.

When you are under the attack of the devil, you must make yourself hungry for the things of God. Think about times you were sick and did not want to eat. What was the first thing someone who cared about you did? They put food in front of you and said, "Eat."

You probably said, "I don't want to eat this. I'm not hungry."

They said, "I don't care. Eat it." Why? Because they knew the nutrients in the food would strengthen your body.

It is the same in the spirit realm. When we are under the fire of the devil, that is not the time to quit going to church. That is not the time to quit reading the Word of God, confessing, and praying. That is not the time to stop our labor for God. Instead, that is the time to turn it up!

Understand that the goal of the enemy is to rid you of your spiritual desire for God. You've got to stay around people who give you life when you are in a war. Don't hang around lifeless, negative, carnal people. Above all, don't isolate yourself. Find someone with spunk and zeal for God. Their influence will help you and strengthen you in a time of trouble. The Bible says a good friend will sharpen you. (See Proverbs 27:17.)

BE STRONG!

Finally, my brethren, be strong in the Lord, and in the power of his might.

Ephesians 6:10

The second thing that happens to a person under attack is a loss of strength. Even though they are smiling and saying the same things, they have lost their unction — their get-up-and-go. They don't have what I call the "bam!" They have lost their spiritual punch and accuracy. There is no life, joy, or jump in them.

True joy, strength, and life come from the inward man. The only way a believer can effectively fight an attack is by gaining strength from the Lord, and the Bible says that the joy of the Lord is our strength (Nehemiah 8:10). We can only get that strength in His presence.

Thou wilt show me the path of life: in thy presence is fullness of joy; at thy right hand there are pleasures for evermore.

Psalm 16:11

Again, we must pray in the Spirit and stay in the Spirit to stay strong. You cannot win outside of the Spirit.

We must be careful not to rely on our natural ability when we are in a spiritual war. When we are more comfortable with natural strengths than we are spiritual strengths, we end up helping the enemy. That is why sometimes, in a church-wide battle, there are disastrous splits, because believers go from spiritual combat into natural combat. Natural combat gets its strength from cutting and slanderous words. Gossip and fear are its weapons.

We must learn to recognize the attack of the enemy in the area of spiritual strength. We must learn to stand and fight with the Word of God and in the realm of the Spirit. If leadership can remain in the Spirit and gain their strength from the Lord, the battle will not be as disastrous.

When the natural body is sick, every part of the body is focused on the attack inside of it. To win in the Spirit, the focus must be the same. When you are under attack, all of your energy must come from the strength you have built in the Lord to overcome it. You must keep your strength up and not grow weak.

Spiritual strength also comes from confessing the Word of God.

Let the weak say, I am strong.

Joel 3:10

The third way to recognize an attack is that you don't feel like yourself. Whining and complaining about the difficulties of our life will only make us feel worse. This negative talk pleases the enemy because it reinforces his work. When our natural body is sick and we feel terrible, we usually gripe and act bossy, even to those we love the most. We tend to lay on the sofa and watch television, or go to bed and sleep the day away.

Also when we are under attack, whether it is totally demonic or maneuvered through another person, we don't feel like our usual self. We begin to feel things that are not true. One of those feelings is paranoia — like we are being judged and criticized for anything we do or say. We feel like we can never please anyone because our life is such a mess. If we give in to those feelings, we'll quit and go backwards.

When those feelings come, we must learn how to reject them. We must stand, resist, and fight back! We should never give in to them and say, "Well, I must just be this way. I'll never do anything for God, because I am no good." If we say that, the enemy has won.

Sometimes we think, "Lord, I'm tired." Spiritual warfare drains our physical body and we have little energy. All we want to do is sit at home and watch television. Don't use the television as an escape. Television isn't wrong, but when we are not spiritually strong, it will only feed our carnal mind and dominate our weak spirit.

Don't hide away in bed all day and pretend the world doesn't exist. Sleep temporarily enables us to escape from reality, but when we wake up, the battle is still there and has possibly gained strength, because we refused to fight.

I had to learn that when I am facing a battle, I can't go to a place where there is no battle going on. That is a retreat. There are no retreats in the kingdom of God — there are only charges! I had to learn to charge forth by proclaiming that God's Word prevailed over anything coming against me — no matter how I felt. When you build your strength in the Lord, you'll have that "charge" no matter what is happening around you.

KNOW WHO YOU ARE

Another major tactic of the enemy is intimidation. Intimidation puts you in a box and you can't come out and be yourself. The devil will try to make you feel insecure because anointed preaching exposes him for what he is. The enemy hates those who know how to walk in the anointing and administer it. The anointing breaks his yoke, his bondage, and his chains. It destroys the lies he has caused people to believe. He knows that once the bondages are broken and you are set free and made strong, you won't take any more garbage from him.

Intimidation makes us feel insecure. Many ministers battle rejection, intimidation, and insecurity. These things hinder them from speaking the truth that sets men free and keep them from operating in God's full anointing. You won't ever be intimidated in a spiritual battle if you know who you are in Christ.

You are the victor; so be it. You are more than a conqueror; so conquer. We are the army of the Lord. We must learn the strategies of the enemy and conquer them. Stand up to the attack, and win in the strength of the Lord.

But ye are a chosen generation, a royal priesthood, an holy nation, a peculiar people; that ye should show forth the praises of him who hath called you out of darkness into his marvellous light.

1 Peter 2:9

We need to memorize this Scripture and recite it daily! We have been delivered from the hands of Satan. Jesus gave His disciples power and authority over all devils. As His royal priesthood, we have been given that same power and authority over every evil thing. Nothing has changed over the past 2,000 years, but we must come to the full realization of the power we do have.

Having power and authority and actually using it are two different things. Spiritual attacks will not go away by themselves. We cannot ignore situations or pretend they don't exist. We have been given the authority not only to stand against the enemy, but to come through it in total victory! Begin to act like you are chosen by God. Begin to act like a royal priest. He has called us to be His disciples, to learn of Him, and then go out and conquer the enemy.

CHAPTER 3

OUR WEAPONS OF WAR

A s we established in chapter one, we must realize that we are not fighting against flesh and blood, but against spiritual wickedness. We can't resist the enemy through natural means. Our weapons must be spiritual.

THE SWORD OF THE SPIRIT

For though we walk in the flesh, we do not war after the flesh:

For the weapons of our warfare are not carnal, but mighty through God to the pulling down of strong holds;

Casting down imaginations, and every high thing that exalteth itself against the knowledge of God, and bringing into captivity every thought to the obedience of Christ.

2 Corinthians 10:3-5

Wherefore take unto you the whole armor of God, that ye may be able to withstand in the evil day, and having done all, to stand.

Stand therefore, having your loins girt about with truth, and having on the breastplate of righteousness;

And your feet shod with the preparation of the gospel of peace;

Above all, taking the shield of faith, wherewith ye shall be able to quench all the fiery darts of the wicked.

And take the helmet of salvation, and the sword of the Spirit, which is the word of God.

Ephesians 6:13-17

The Word of God must be strong in you at all times. It is your security. The only thing that wounds the enemy is the sword of the Spirit, or the Word of God, and the "sword" denotes action on your part. No matter how beat up and drained you feel, you are equipped for action with the Word of God.

The Greek word for **take** means *strength*, "as the thrust of a ram." (See James Strong's, *The Exhaustive Concordance of the Bible*, Nashville: Abingdon, 1890, "Greek Dictionary of the New Testament," #142.) We could say the verse this way: "Gather a thrusting strength to yourself through the Word of God, so you may be able to oppose an attack by overcoming it and establishing yourself."

Cast not away therefore your confidence, which hath great recompence of reward.

Hebrews 10:35

The Word of God is our confidence. If we cling to it and make it a part of us, our reward will be great. When it comes down to a brutal attack, we must fight against it with brutal trust in the Lord. The devil will try to convince us that God is not going to do anything for us and we're not going to make it, but God's Word says otherwise. We must choose to believe His Word. We must make a conscious choice to keep our confidence and not cast away what belongs to us. We can't wait for an emotional outburst. We can't wait for a personal prophecy or a minister to lay hands on us. We can't wait for a visit from heaven. God didn't call us "weak-kneed babies," He called us soldiers. Just choose to believe. Get in there and believe the Word!

We've got to be aggressive with the Word of God and allow it to work for us. Christians who wait without action will never receive what is theirs. Ruthlessly believe the Word of God. Run out to meet it.

Miracles, signs, and wonders are wonderful and bring many to Christ, but they won't sustain us through the enemy's attacks. We must live by faith, and faith comes by hearing the Word of God. (See Romans 10:17.) Living by faith causes God's destiny to come to you. If all you can do is read one verse of Scripture and say, "God, I believe that," *then do it*. That is aggressive faith. Don't feel guilty about that. It doesn't matter if the devil has stolen almost everything you have. Choose to believe the promises God made to you through His Word. If you are doing all that you can, then keep doing it. New strength will come and you will win.

Holding to the Word is not complicated; it is maintaining the will to dig into it that is hard under an attack. Just remember, no matter what it looks like in the natural, if you will hold to that thread of belief until more strength comes, you will make it. Faith is not 3,000 confessions. Sometimes there's just enough time to say, "I believe."

Do not let the enemy speak lies to your mind. Fire back at him with the scriptures you know. We shut the mouths of lions with the Word of God. Instead of a roar, you'll hear a whimpering retreat. The devil is afraid of the strength in the Spirit. He is intimidated by strong believers. So scare him!

When you unite yourself with the Word of God, God can effectively use the rest of His weapons of war through you.

PSALMS, HYMNS, AND SPIRITUAL SONGS

And be not drunk with wine, wherein is excess; but be filled with the Spirit;

Speaking to yourselves in psalms and hymns and spiritual songs, singing and making melody in your heart to the Lord.

Ephesians 5:18,19

Praise and worship causes you to have an understanding of the greatness, the almightiness, and the awesomeness of God. It is your strength in the midst of an attack. Praise and worship gives you a God-consciousness and keeps your mind stayed on Him.

We don't have to wait for the church music leader to lead us into praise and worship. We can make music in our heart, by ourselves. If that doesn't come easily, then go to the book of Psalms and let those anointed words minister to you.

We find that in every situation David experienced, God delivered him from them all and showed Himself strong. David knew what it was like to be surrounded by evil. He had been betrayed by trusted friends. He had faced every obstacle that could come to a man, yet his response was, **I will bless the Lord at all times: his praise shall continually be in my mouth** (Psalm 34:1).

The Psalms are explicit in describing the way we can feel about certain situations without condemnation. It's called "being real with God." Every time we are real with God and cry out to Him, He shows His strength to us. Praise unto God strengthened David and encouraged him.

The Psalms, just like the rest of the Word, have a continual anointing upon them. I've written several down that have ministered and have put my own melody to them. Sometimes, because they are in me so deeply, a song will burst out that has been in my heart.

One of my staff will look at me and say, "Where did that come from?"

I have learned to say, "It's good! Sing unto the Lord!" Those songs come from our spirit to give us life and encouragement. Many times we'll receive our answer when we are praising and worshipping God. Don't be embarrassed. Your own ears need to hear it!

You may say, "Well, I just don't know if that is necessary." But we are *commanded* to praise the Lord.

Rejoice in the Lord, O ye righteous: for praise is come-
ly for the upright.

Psalm 33:1

Praise ye the Lord. Praise ye the name of the Lord;
praise him O ye servants of the Lord.

Psalm 135:1

O give thanks unto the Lord; for he is good: for his
mercy endureth for ever.

Psalm 136:1

Praise ye the Lord. Sing unto the Lord a new song, and
his praise in the congregation of saints.

Let them praise his name in the dance: let them sing
praises unto him with the timbrel and harp.

Psalm 149:1,3

Line yourself up with the Word of God by praising and worshipping God. Through your spirit, the Holy Spirit will witness and
speak to you. Many times, when you are singing to God, He will
begin to sing right out of you and give you an answer.

I can remember when I was in my worst war, songs would start
way down deep in me. A song would be just a small little voice. I kept
giving place to it and by the end of the day, it would come out real
bold. Sometimes, even when I would ache, the songs of the Spirit
would still come. I would sing for hours. I would say over and over,
"God, I believe in You." It did not matter what was happening
around me. Sometimes, I would write the things that were inside of
me. That's what David and others did in Psalms. They wrote the
melodies inside of them for others to see and receive life. That is
what hymns are: written melodies from hearts crying out and rejoicing to God, proclaiming Him as Lord despite the battles.

Don't be afraid to pour your heart out to God. Cleansing comes
when we do that. The devil tells you, "If you say what you really feel,

that is doubt." God understands you and knows how you feel anyway. Sometimes you have to have that release to get the garbage out of you.

As believers, we can sometimes get so caught up in the mechanics of faith, we forget the character of God. In all of your journeys, in all of your battles, in all of your situations, always remember to come to Jesus, He receives. He doesn't cast you out. No matter where you are, no matter what you look like, if you come believing, you are accepted. The mercy and strength of God will restore you back to where you belong.

When you make melody from your heart, life will come from heaven and keep you going. If you don't have life, you don't win. Read the book of Psalms, and let those anointed words carry you out into the blessedness of the Spirit. Then, just catch up to it and sing your own songs.

Paul encouraged us to do praise always; Moses and Miriam praised God as they saw the victory at the Red Sea; and David praised God when he was in the midst of war. Those are just three examples we need to learn from and practice today. When your church is in a war, when you are under attack and feel you are getting weak, then one thing you need to do is let the songs of the Spirit come out of your mouth. Let them soar and sing them loud.

Make your head take account. Make your head line up and listen to what your spirit is saying. Your whole war may just be in your head, and the words of the Spirit will soothe your mind. The songs of the Spirit will cause peace to overcome disturbing thoughts, a disturbed body, and a disturbed heart. Songs of the Spirit cause peace in the midst of a great storm. They will give you the strength to continue and win the battle. They will bring your soul back into common sense so it can be renewed. They will restore your position in the Spirit.

Praise and worship is a "traveling vehicle." It will cause you to travel into the good things of the Lord and to have an understanding of the greatness, the almightiness, and the awesomeness of God.

When you sing and worship from your heart, He comes down. (See John 4:23). Praise and worship is a balance for you during attack. Many times during a battle, and it seems as if God is nowhere, these songs will restore your consciousness of God.

You don't have to wait until you are in church where there are musical instruments. You don't have to have a music leader. You do exactly what the Scripture says. You make music in your heart, by yourself. If it sounds dead and dry, go back to the book of Psalms and read some more. Stay there and allow your heart to be put back in position. Soon you will begin to get encouraged. You will begin to sing about your situation, about the problems, and many times the Lord will cause the answer to sing out of you. The songs of the Lord are a weapon.

Out of the mouth of babes and sucklings hast thou ordained strength because of thine enemies, that thou mightest still the enemy and the avenger.

Psalm 8:2

Praise and worship stops the condemnation and onslaught of the enemy in our life.

When I took my first trip to Africa, I went into the communist nation of Mozambique. They were in war and didn't like Americans too well, but I felt led of the Lord to go, so I obeyed and went.

I had felt in my spirit that I would encounter some type of military action on my way into the country. As I entered in from Zimbabwe, I was amazed at all the destruction. I just sat there and prayed protection scriptures over myself.

With no mishap, I preached in a little grass hut Assembly of God church that night and slept in the church when the service was over. The next day everything was going in a normal manner. I thought, "Well, maybe my meditation of the Word and continual praying stopped everything. Maybe I was supposed to pray and prevent." So, I forgot about it and climbed in the back of an old truck taking me back to Zimbabwe.

I fell asleep in the back of that truck, and suddenly awoke to gun-fire. Someone yelled, "Get out of the truck!" Being young and not used to that kind of situation, I stood up and looked around. I thought the bullets flying over my head were meant for someone else — not me!

I finally realized those bullets were meant for me and I had better take cover. I ran into a ditch, laid down, and prayed. Up to that time, John Wayne movies were about the extent of my military awareness. I didn't really know what was going on and how dangerous it actually was until after we got back in the truck — then I got scared. I remember telling my angels that if I died, they were getting it on the way up!

When it was all over, several people had been shot and some died.

As I continued my trip to Zimbabwe, I began to worship and pray. I kept saying to the Lord, "I thought a good man's steps were ordered by the Lord. Did I miss it?" As I kept plugging heaven for an answer, a song of worship rose up within me and I spent the next thirty minutes praising and worshipping the Lord. As I began to sing, I felt an over-whelming sense of divine protection all around me. I knew that no matter what situation I found myself in, I was assured of His deliverance.

There are times when you can sing in tongues by choice and times when you can sing in your natural language by choice. But there are also times when the Holy Spirit will give you an unction and it will come out in both tongues and natural language. You can tell the difference. It has more force to it when it comes by the Spirit. When the gifts of the Spirit come to you this way, you don't have to have someone to interpret; you can interpret yourself.

That is what happened to me that day. As I began to sing, the Lord began to speak right out of me. He began to speak the answer and the causes back to me. He told me of His protection and His purpose. That song came right up out of me and satisfied my soul, my flesh, and my spirit. I was at peace with what happened that day, and it never bothered me again.

I will agree it is difficult to praise and worship during times of attack. But when we are under fire, we need to bring out the biggest spiritual gun we have and blast the enemy. Remember, praise stills the avenger! Begin to praise and worship the Lord from your heart. Put yourself in remembrance of how great God is. He is bigger than any problem you face.

FORGIVENESS

To whom ye forgive any thing, I forgive also: for if I forgave any thing, to whom I forgave it, for your sakes forgave I it in the person of Christ;

Lest Satan should get an advantage of us: for we are not ignorant of his devices.

2 Corinthians 2:10,11

Unforgiveness is a primary device of the enemy. Therefore, one of our greatest weapons against Satan is to walk in forgiveness. Forgiveness proves we know our God and our enemy. It puts our focus and trust in the right direction. It allows the power, strength, and might of the Holy Spirit to operate in our life.

Bitterness, resentment, and unforgiveness place us in the middle of strife, envy, revenge, confusion, illness, and double-mindedness. Bitterness is a never-ending cycle that will eventually take our life. Forgiveness gives us life.

If we have been wronged by another person, we must forgive them. No matter how hard it is, we need to speak forgiveness out of our mouth — our heart will eventually follow the words we speak. It is only after we forgive that our prayers can be effectual and fervent, availing much.

On the other hand, unforgiveness will lead to pride. If we have been attacked in the area of self-worth, or if we have been rejected, we have a tendency to counteract by exalting ourselves. Pride that has seasoned itself from hurts and wounds deceives us into thinking we are winning and gaining ground, when in reality we are steadily losing the glory of God in our lives. Keep in mind that the enemy can trick us into pride even when we think we are serving God.

I have seen minister after minister fall to this deception. They have been repeatedly challenged in their doctrine, their stand for God, and in their personal lives. As a result, instead of staying pliable to the correcting voice of the Lord, they develop a shell of pride and enter into what I call "the persecution complex." They think they are right no matter what comes their way. If you disagree with them, they think you have a devil. They think everyone is out to get them. Instead of hearing the voice of the Lord, they submit to a lifestyle of constant and self-induced persecution. In their defense, they will even pervert Scripture. They eventually think that if you are not under constant attack, you are doing nothing for God.

The late Kathryn Kuhlman was constantly attacked in her ministry from religious leaders, friends, the media, and a personal mistake, but she never reacted in pride. She never took on a "persecution complex," although she had natural reason to do so. Even in the time she personally stumbled, she regained her strength in a way that should teach us all. Her ministry retained such a presence of God that even when she walked into the television studios, her presence could be felt. Despite the multitudes healed and saved in her services, no one left looking at Miss Kuhlman. God took her from glory to glory, worldwide, despite the persecution and attacks.

The basic principle remains the same. Miss Kuhlman said over and over in her ministry, "I know where I came from, and I know better than anyone else what makes this ministry what it is. It's certainly not Kathryn Kuhlman."

That's the way we are to be. We cannot let unforgiveness gain entrance into our spirit man. We are to make ourselves available to be used of God, despite the attacks. It is not our ability nor our intellect that works the victory, it is the working of the Holy Spirit through a clean vessel.

STAYING HUMBLE

God resisteth the proud, but giveth grace unto the humble.

Submit yourselves therefore to God. Resist the devil, and he will flee from you.

James 4:6,7

It may be true that we are seasoned and mature. We may know many things according to the Word of God, but to be effective, we must be strong in *all* areas of the Word, not just a portion of it. Emphasizing just a portion of the Word, feeding on those truths alone, and refusing to submit to the whole counsel of God will cause us to fall. We cannot point a condemning finger at the world, then pervert a spiritual truth by thinking we are absolutely "invincible."

We cannot arrogantly attack everything that hits us and still hear the voice of the Lord first and foremost. It may be our own correction that will cause us to win the battle. To effectively go through an attack, we must examine our heart, our life, our trust, and our focus in order to win and stay accurate.

If we live in the Spirit, let us also walk in the Spirit.

Galatians 5:25

As ye have therefore received Christ Jesus the Lord, so walk ye in him:

Rooted and built up in him, and stablished in the faith as ye have been taught, abounding therein with thanksgiving.

Beware lest any man spoil you through philosophy and vain deceit, after the tradition of men, after the rudiments of the world, and not after Christ.

For in him dwelleth all the fullness of the Godhead bodily.

Colossians 2:6-9

We must not think we are a "special breed" because we are anointed and called. "Special breeds" are deceived into thinking they have all the knowledge they need. They get out on their own with what little they know, and they fall. Only by having Christ in us, walking in His righteousness, and being rooted in the Word of God are we able to stay humble.

Confess to one another therefore your faults — your slips, your false steps, your offenses, your sins; and pray [also] for one another, that you may be healed and restored — to a spiritual tone of mind and heart. The earnest (heartfelt, continued) prayer of a righteous man makes tremendous power available — dynamic in its working.

James 5:16 AMP

Sometimes we focus so keenly on the latter part of that verse, we forget the first part of it. It is only *after* we forgive that our prayers can be effectual and fervent, availing much. How can a prayer be heard by God and produce great results, if it is prayed from a heart filled with bitterness and revenge? If we live and walk in the Spirit, there is no room for offense and bitterness.

FERVENT PRAYER

It doesn't matter how feeble or weak we feel. Jesus sees our hearts. When we're under attack, any prayer we offer to God out of a pure heart will produce results. Sometimes we think we have to groan and travail for hours to get results, but prayer is not that complicated. Prayer is simply talking to God. It is not a formula or a ritual. I like what my grandmother says when people say they can't pray. She answers, "Well, you can talk to your father, can't you? Talk to God the same way." When I am under a heavy attack, I know that even my thoughts toward God count as a prayer to Him.

"Fervent" does not mean *scared faith*. Scared faith is a little bit of fear mixed with a little bit of faith. Scared faith doesn't work — fervent prayer works. It doesn't matter how small your faith may seem; just stay fervent in it.

Prayer during an attack starts from the same source as any other spiritual arena; it comes by choice. It takes what I call "willpower" to grab hold of all three parts — spirit, soul, and body — and make yourself go into prayer concerning your situation. During a spiritual attack, chaos hits. Everything, both inside and outside of you, is out of order. It takes an active decision on your part to pull yourself back in line.

A person who has not made that decision will face three directions. They won't know which way to go or what to believe. They can go the body way, and try to forget their problems through the flesh. Or they can go the mind way, and live in paranoia and confusion. Or, they can choose the spirit's way and pull everything back in its proper arena.

Spiritual attacks will paralyze you. They try to frighten you by worry and fear, frustrating you into doing nothing. As a result, your body will not obey you, your mind will talk you out of the right way or into the wrong way and you'll fall. A kingdom divided cannot stand. The devil defeats you by dividing you.

When you are under an attack, don't be frustrated if it feels like your prayer doesn't get past the ceiling. Have enough faith to believe God reached down and got it. If we get condemned by thinking our prayers didn't go anywhere, we'll give up. Remember, God hears the earnest, heartfelt prayers of a righteous man.

Fervent prayer is focused. The mind cannot properly focus on a variety of things at one time, so don't let your situation overwhelm you. Start with the most important thing to you, the first priority and fervently pray and believe God for the answer. It doesn't matter if all the details of the situation are intertwined, start with the most important detail and stick to that one. The answer will come, because you have the faith to believe for it. As soon as the peace comes, move on and deal with the next situation.

In fervent prayer your spirit, soul, and body are as one, united in the purpose of God to see His plan fulfilled — His will done. Your spirit is your source of prayer, and your soul (desires, emotions, imaginations, memories) and body (actions) work together in submission to your spirit.

And Jesus knew their thoughts, and said unto them, Every kingdom divided against itself is brought to desolation; and every city or house divided against itself shall not stand.

Matthew 12:25

As individuals, we are a *kingdom* consisting of a spirit, soul, and body. Therefore, you are not a mind. You are a *spirit* that owns a *mind* that lives in a *body*. If these three parts of your kingdom are divided, you'll fall. If your mind is thinking carnal thoughts, your body is sitting in church, and your spirit is not leading them, you're divided. A kingdom divided cannot stand. The devil defeats us by dividing us.

We must *choose* to keep our kingdom united. A person who doesn't will not know which way to go or what to believe. They try to solve their problems by appeasing the flesh, they let their mind rule and live in paranoia and confusion — or they choose to be led by the Holy Spirit and keep their *kingdom* united.

Another equally important part of fervent prayer has to do with speaking in tongues. When we are under a heavy spiritual attack, we're limited by our natural language. So God has given us a Helper in times of trouble — the Holy Spirit.

Likewise the Spirit also helpeth our infirmities: for we know not what we should pray for as we ought: but the Spirit itself maketh intercession for us with groanings which cannot be uttered.

And he that searcheth the hearts knoweth what is the mind of the Spirit, because he maketh intercession for the saints according to the will of God.

Romans 8:26,27

Our own mind is limited and cannot always speak what it should. This scripture says that God's Holy Spirit, dwelling inside the believer, is always there to lead us in the right direction. He will come to our aid, energize us, and pray through us to bring about the perfect will of God for our situation.

The Greek word for **intercession** means, "superior to, very chiefest, very highly, of necessity, to reign." (See *Strong's Concordance,* #5228.) Fervent prayer is not something we can muster up through a planned emotion, but rather comes through the unction of the Holy Spirit.

Strong spiritual tongues have a vital place in the believer's life. When we have said everything we know to say from our natural minds, the Holy Spirit will pray the highest form of prayer through us by words that cannot be articulated. The Spirit of God knows the will of God in every situation. When we allow Him to pray through us, the guidance, wisdom, and direction we need will be supplied.

Groanings of the spirit can only come by the Holy Spirit's unction, not from a preplanned emotion. The Old Testament speaks of God answering and delivering the people of Israel as He heard their groanings. But these human groanings of grief and despair were only symbolic of the manifestations of the Spirit of God spoken of in the book of Romans. We must be careful not to get into works of the flesh when we deal with a spiritual situation.

The cleansing of our hearts in repentance, knowledge of the Word of God, and the understanding of what strong prayer can do will lead us into total victory every time. The Spirit of God is always ready and willing to link up with us and pray the perfect will of God in every situation.

SAYING *NO* TO CONTROLLING POWERS

A few years ago the world discovered a valuable word: *no.* The secular media made *no* a household word by popularizing the "Just Say No" drug campaign. That slogan was advertised on television, radio, billboards, and in magazines and newspapers in an effort to keep young people from drugs.

However, it is time the body of Christ rediscovered this very important, priceless word, this small but very powerful word. After all, God was the first to advocate the concept for which the word stands — denying Satan and the bondage others seek to hold us in.

Every preacher and every lay person needs to learn to say *no*. In fact, every human being needs to learn to say *no*. Undoubtedly, we have all been in a situation where we wished we had said *no* instead of *yes*. However, because we had given our word, we went ahead and did whatever we had committed to. Perhaps saying *yes* not only led to inconvenience, but to sin. We did not sin by breaking our word, but by grumbling and complaining or by criticizing and finding fault. Perhaps we sinned by falling into resentment, bitterness, or unforgiveness toward another person.

How do we know when to say *no*? Sometimes a *yes* or *no* answer isn't the most obvious thing in the world. Many people seem to be afraid to say *no*. They seem to equate *no* with negative things — like having no fun or joy in life. Nothing could be farther from the truth.

Restore unto me the joy of thy salvation.
Psalm 51:12

Christians should have joy, vitality, and fun in whatever they do. If there is no joy, something is very wrong. They are not walking in God's presence, because there is joy in His presence.

Every now and then we need to check up on our joy and peace gauges as we drive down the road called "life." If those gauges are on empty, we need to get refilled. We should not let our joy and peace run low.

Phyllis Mackall, a precious friend, once told me, "There are two things every person in the ministry needs to learn to say: *no* and *thank you*."

Her advice is both wise and true. If we say *yes* when it should have been *no*, we get into trouble. And when we forget to show appreciation to people, we cause trouble and hurt. Everyone needs to say no more often.

How often have you said *no* and gotten into trouble? Usually, more trouble comes from saying *yes*. We need to learn to say *no* without feeling guilty about it. Sometimes *no* is God's anointed answer for a situation.

BOLDLY SAYING *NO*

If you begin saying no, soon you will know how to say it and smile. No is a wonderful word. Phyllis helped me learn the value of that little, powerful word. I would go over to Phyllis' house and she would say, "Roberts, what's the anointed word?"

I would say, "No."

And she would say, "That's not loud enough. That's not strong enough. You don't believe it quite yet. Say it again."

She would have me say it over and over until it came out loud, strong, and bold.

"That's it. You've got it," she would finally say.

Sometimes we have to yell something until it becomes a part of our heart. If we speak softly, what we say seems to carry no weight even with our own self. Learn to say *no* boldly. A weak *no* can too easily be turned into a *yes*.

As an example, when a child sees a toy they want in the department store, they will often beg and plead with their parents to buy that toy for them. Depending on how boldly the parent says *no*, the child continues until they feel they have a definite answer. A good strong *no* can usually quiet the child. However, a weak *no* will bring on more pleading until the parent gives in and changes their *no* to a *yes*.

The same is true in our spiritual lives. When we say a strong, bold *no* to the devil, he will flee from us. Our attitude cannot be, "Satan, I really wish you would leave me alone. I am so tired of you controlling me." No! Our answer must be, "Satan, I command you to leave me alone, in the name of Jesus. I will not succumb to this temptation you have placed before me. I will not allow you to control my life."

THE FIRST NO

Adam and Eve said *yes* when they should have said *no* and suffered serious consequences as a result. (See Genesis 3.)

God told Adam and Eve, "You can eat from any tree except one."

Then the serpent came along and tried to turn God's *no* into a *yes*. He told Eve the fruit was good for her, because it would make her just like God.

Instead of yelling *no* at the devil, Eve began to think, "Well, that fruit does look good. God could not have *really* meant for us not to eat of it."

Yes, He did. When God says *no*, He means *no*. When He says *yes*, He means *yes*. But Eve ate of the fruit and gave some to Adam, who then had his chance to say *no* and turn things around. But Adam put Eve before God and joined her in eating the fruit. The consequence was that they were separated from the presence of God. No longer could they have daily, intimate communion with Him.

If Adam and Eve had obeyed God's first *no*, they would still be in the Garden of Eden, eating, having fun, and enjoying life. They could have continued to live in perfect joy. Instead, they ate the fruit and were miserable — the state of all those who say *yes* when they should have said *no*. Success is not built on how many times you say *yes*. Usually, success is built on how many times you say a strong *no* — and stick to it. A weak *no* too easily can be turned into a *yes*.

Was God being mean? Certainly not. His prohibition was for their own protection. God has His children's best interests in mind when He says no. *No* from the Father is often a word of protection for our personal life, our family, our business, our church, and our nation.

THE POWER OF *NO*

No has legs. It is a force that *runs* from the appearance of evil. Those who say *no* do not walk with the ungodly, stand with sinners, nor sit with those who are scornful of God's ways. (See Psalm 1:1.) *No* never stays in a place where evil abounds.

No has actions and a big voice. If we do not do what we know to do, we have sinned. (See James 4:17.) Not saying *no* when we know to do so, is sin.

Often, *no* is very hard to say, but once we have said it, we will feel like a giant. We'll be happy and feel God's pleasure inside us. *No* stops conflicts of doubt and guilt. *No* has no suspicion in it.

No is a universal word. Even where people do not speak English, they know what *no* means — which can be very important when you are traveling abroad!

A missionary friend of mine is alive today because she stood on God's Word and said *no*. Late one night, alone in a foreign country, she found herself surrounded by ten men. Great fear attempted to engulf her, because she knew those men were attracted by her blonde hair and fair skin, and they meant her no good.

Everything inside her was screaming to run, but she knew there was no way she could outrun them all. She remembered two Scripture verses, **Greater is he that is in you, than he that is in the world** (1 John 4:4), and **No weapon that is formed against thee shall prosper** (Isaiah 54:17).

She pointed to one of the men and said out loud, bold and strong, "*No*, no you don't! Move out of my way. In Jesus' name, get out of my way. I am coming through."

At first, the men just stood there leering at her.

Then she pointed her finger and said, "In Jesus' name, move, NOW."

One man bowed to her and motioned her through, so she walked on past the men. When she got around the corner, she ran for her life!

No protected her. She stood on the name of Jesus and on His Word and declared a strong *no*. The devil is out to destroy us, but if we rise up and boldly declare *no* to ungodly things, he cannot harm us. It is time believers stand up to the devil and proclaim a bold *no*.

NO HAS BACKBONE

One of the things my grandmother used to say to me is, "Any old dead fish can float down the river, but it takes one with backbone to swim up the river against the current."

No is part of our spiritual backbone. God did not make us to be spineless jellyfish, He made us in His image, and God has a backbone. It does not take a backbone to go with the flow of people's ideas, thoughts, and opinions. If they are wrong, we need to realize God made us with a backbone, and we can say *no*.

We are made in God's image, so we also can say *no* at the proper time and place.

NO MAKES ENEMIES

Many people are not used to hearing *no* in today's permissive society, and they do not like it. That is why a lot of people do not use the word more often — no one likes enemies. We all like to be liked. However, I would rather say *no* and be obedient to the Lord than not say it and disobey. We must stand on God's truth and declare *no* when it should be *no*, and *yes* when it should be *yes*.

Second Peter 2 tells us that in these last days, many will be deceived by false teachers and false doctrines. The Bible says that even some of "the elect" will go astray. (See 2 Peter 2:15). Why? They have not learned to say no. Those who will not be deceived will be fought by those who are deceived.

Saying *no* to the doctrines and operations of the enemy causes some people to become your enemies — some will not like you, and some may hate you. But do not waver. Keep saying *no*, because **if God be for us, who can be against us?** (Romans 8:31).

We have seen how the Word of God, our praise and worship unto Him, walking in forgiveness, the cleansing of our hearts, the understanding of fervent prayer, and saying no to the enemy will lead us into total victory every time. Use every weapon God has provided for you and win the battle, in Jesus' name. You have been powerfully equipped by God. Now go forth and conquer!

CHAPTER 4

CONTROLLING POWERS OVER THE SPIRIT

O ur spirit man is the direct channel between God and ourselves. We receive instruction, direction, and purpose from Him through our spirit man. We follow the unction of the Holy Spirit in our spirit and direct our lives from the guidance and warnings we sense from it.

The spirit man is what makes us who we are. It is the highest creative power inside of us. We were created spirit first, then body and soul. Our mind and our body are pieces of "equipment" that are needed in order for our spirit to carry out the purpose of God in the earth. God does not talk to a piece of equipment — our mind. He speaks to our heart — our spirit man.

The plans of heaven come to us through our spirit. Our mind may find out a few seconds later and be able to interpret what our spirit has received. This is why our spirit sometimes knows something, but we are not able to put it into words — our mind has not yet comprehended it.

Our spirit man is an individual. Each spirit man has a different call and a different purpose to make the body of Christ complete. Our spirit man is unlimited in potential as it feeds and nurtures itself from the Word of God.

The spirit of man is the candle of the Lord.

Proverbs 20:27

Our spirit man is the light of God to the world. That is why the spirit must affect our soul and our body. The Bible does not say our emotions or our flesh are the light of the world. Matthew 5:14 says *we* are the light of the world. Our soul and body reflect Jesus inside of us.

Although being filled with Jesus helps us become the light to the world, it is still our choice whether or not to let it shine. If we are going to live in the Spirit, we must learn to also walk in the Spirit. (See Galatians 5:25.)

We must learn how to let the Holy Spirit direct our spirit man and understand the longing our spirit man has for Him. We must learn the character of God Himself. We must learn how to abide by His spirit and not quench His actions. We must learn to base our decisions upon the unction within us and follow it. As we discipline our spirit, we will become "strong in spirit" and useful for the purpose of God.

ATTACK ON THE SPIRIT MAN

The enemy's purpose is to keep us from expressing Jesus to the world, so he tries first for the soul and body of man. But when a person is spiritual, and the body and soul are totally subject to their spirit, then the attack will hit the spirit man immediately. If a person is ignorant of the devices of the enemy, they will easily succumb to his tactics.

Is it possible for a man to have his body and soul subjected to the Word of God and still be ignorant of the attack on his spirit? Yes! Even while disciplining our flesh and soul, if we have lost our joy, our liberty of expression, and our spiritual perceptions, then our spirit is under attack. If our plans or activities keep us from a deeper relationship with God, it is from the enemy. It doesn't matter how good it seems or how much potential there is for a great work. If our fellowship with God decreases because of it, it is not from Him. To fulfill our true purpose from God, we must rely on a constant relationship with Him to complete it.

Our righteousness can also be attacked. Some of the most sincere believers, adamantly trying to renew their minds in the area of body and soul, have lost their sense of righteousness. They meditate on feelings of unworthiness and discipline their body and soul on this basis. What was once an exciting spiritual frontier has now become a "rut," and they have lost their vision.

Take time to invest in your spirit man. Not only will it cause you to fulfill the destiny for your life, but the end results will bring maturity into every life you meet.

ABUSIVE CONTROL OF THE SPIRIT

The area of spiritual control, or manipulation, is by far the most dangerous, because it treads on the spiritual principles of heaven. It is dangerous for both the controller and the one being controlled because it treads on the spiritual principles of heaven.

Spiritual manipulation is based on the soulish realm. It has nothing to do with the true spiritual realm, but uses a *spiritual principle* as its primary tool.

We discussed the attributes of an abusive controller in chapter one, and we can see why such a person would revert to spiritual manipulation. If an individual cannot control another person through emotions, he will resort to spiritual manipulation to keep his victim subservient to him. Spiritual manipulators have not developed godly character in a particular area. They are led by their lust or desire for control rather than by the Spirit of God. We most often find these types of people in the local church.

A bishop then must be blameless....

Not a novice, lest being lifted up with pride he fall into the condemnation of the devil.

1 Timothy 3:2,6

Paul wrote this passage to warn Timothy against allowing a young, inexperienced convert to assume the responsibilities of spiritual leadership. Paul knew the danger of promoting the spiritually immature too quickly. Such people often fall prey to the temptation of pride. They tend to get "puffed up" if they are given a high position in the church. Instead of humbly serving the body of Christ, they become pious and manipulative.

Then there are those upon whom God has truly bestowed a special anointing or gift. Again, if they have not fully matured, such people feel they are among the elite and carry an air of superiority about them. They look down on others whom they consider "less spiritual," and often use or abuse those under their authority, rather than loving and caring for them. They fail to recognize that a strong, godly character helps their gift and anointing to operate at its fullest potential and to last a lifetime. Those who don't concentrate on building a strong character may lose what gift and anointing they have been given.

God has no *superstars*, He only has *servants*. If a servant does his job, God will promote him. But no matter how great his name may become, a true servant will still have a desire to meet the needs of the people in his charge. That is the purpose of a ministry gift. A true servant must be careful not to use his God-given authority to "lord over" others.

God is a personal God who speaks to the hearts of men and women individually. Believers who are in leadership roles must be particularly careful to say exactly what the Lord tells them to say — nothing more and nothing less! Leaders have a responsibility to make certain that when they say that something is of God, it really is. They do this by spending time in prayer, searching the Scriptures, and seeking seasoned, godly counsel.

BEWARE OF THE SUPER-SPIRITUAL

In every church there are members who think everyone should obey them, because they have been there the longest or because they are the most spiritual. Such people will either seek to dominate the leadership in every decision made, or they will give their advice on every personal circumstance among the members.

Do not base your life on the opinions of another person, especially if that individual has not been ordained by God for leadership. Judge everything you hear by the Word of God.

The Spirit itself beareth witness with our spirit, that we are the children of God.

Romans 8:16

We will know the voice of the Lord by our inner witness, not by the feelings or opinions of others.

Beware of the following warning signs of an abusive controller:

• They want to organize a Bible study without the pastor's blessing, because "the pastor does not teach the *deep* things of the Spirit." Not only does this spell trouble (especially if you are the one chosen to lead this special Bible study), this kind of behavior usually leads to a church split.

   Don't fall prey to this type of spiritual delusion. If it is time for you to be in a position of leadership, God will put you there. He will motivate the pastor to invite you to lead a segment of the body of Christ — under his supervision — if that is God's plan. Take your training very seriously, and do not allow yourself to be pushed out ahead of God's timetable by an ambitious controller who wants to take the credit for your success.

• They give out false words from the Lord or false prophecies. Usually such words or visions are either extremely morbid, or extremely favorable. They are designed for the same purpose — to push the hearer out ahead of God's timing and ultimately abort the call of God upon his life.

People who give out such words and visions have not had a visitation from God. Beware of giving heed to such self-styled "prophets." When it comes to your personal call, why would God speak something to someone else that He has not already shared with you? Personal prophecies and visions concerning another person are to be a *confirmation* of what the individual already knows in his heart. If another person can entirely lead your life through prophecies and visions, you will never be a leader for God.

Therefore thus says the Lord of hosts concerning the prophets: Behold, I will feed them with [the bitterness of] wormwood, and make them drink the [poisonous] water of gall; for from the [false] prophets of Jerusalem profaneness and ungodliness have gone forth into all the land.

Thus says the Lord of hosts, Do not listen to the words of the [false] prophets who prophesy to you. They teach you vanity — emptiness, falsity and futility — and fill you with vain hopes; they speak a vision of their own minds, and not from the mouth of the Lord.

Jeremiah 23:15,16 AMP

The Word of God is very strong against false prophecies and visions. The false prophets in Jeremiah's day prophesied out of their own hearts. Do not fall into the trap of receiving false "words" or "visions." To be a leader who follows God, you must know the Lord for yourself in order to hear His plan for your life and to follow His perfect timing.

The devil wants to destroy your calling and thwart your purpose in the earth. His plan of attack will be based on your weaknesses. He will attempt to execute that plan in the way that you least expect, and he will succeed unless you are sensitive to the Spirit of God.

- They act very spiritual. They act as though they are spiritual people, but in reality their control is of the devil. Often "super-spiritual" people watch for those whom they can spiritually manipulate or spiritually control. If you have a specific call upon your life, they will recognize it and single you out for their "special ministry." Many times such people are unseasoned themselves, so they will give you "words from the Lord" that will push you out ahead of God's perfect timing. If you are led more strongly by ambition than by the Spirit of God, you will fall for such illusions. Many genuine calls upon people's lives have been aborted because of super-spiritual, abusive controllers.

CONTROLLING PRAYERS

Another variation of spiritual manipulation is *controlling prayers*. Controlling prayers are born from worry, frustration, and flesh. A person who prays controlling prayers may act spiritual, but if they pray from their desire rather than from their spirit, they will not succeed.

Can Christians pray controlling prayers? Certainly, they can! But if misused, these prayers are a form of witchcraft! Remember: Words are spiritual weapons.

A controlling prayer is harmful and misused when it violates or dominates another person's will. It is composed of words with a spiritual force behind them, spoken to influence the course of another's life. The only time a controlling prayer should be used by a Christian is when the Word of God is used against the enemy. Jesus explained this method of prayer.

And I will give unto thee the keys of the kingdom of heaven: and whatsoever thou shalt bind on earth shall be bound in heaven: and whatsoever thou shalt loose on earth shall be loosed in heaven.

Matthew 16:19

However, an abusive controller prays their own fleshly desires for someone else out of their own human heart. They try to make the other individual obey their selfish desires, rather than the Lord's will for that person's life. The person praying may or may not understand that they are loosing evil influences.

In Matthew 12, Jesus had just healed a man possessed with a blind and mute evil spirit. The people murmured among themselves, for they could not believe the miracle they had just witnessed. In response, Jesus taught them about the power of words.

For by your words you will be justified and acquitted, and by your words you will be condemned and sentenced.

Matthew 12:37 AMP

With our words we can bless or curse. Controlling prayer falls under the category of a curse, because they are words spoken against another person in an attempt to satisfy selfish human desires.

An example of a controlling prayer is the one prayed by a mother who wanted her daughter to marry a certain young man — one who was already married! She prayed that the young married couple would get a divorce so the husband would "see the light" and marry her daughter. Because of this mother's unceasing soulish prayers, trouble was sent into this marriage by her words. Finally, the couple became aware of the situation. They rose up and broke the power of the words spoken against them in the spirit realm and their marriage continued to prosper.

Selfish, controlling prayers can occur in any area of life where human desire is placed above the will of God.

Delight thyself also in the Lord; and he shall give thee the desires of thine heart.

Psalm 37:4

This is one of the most commonly misquoted scriptures in the Bible. I cannot count how many times I have heard this verse quoted by Christians who have placed their own desires above the will of God — and expected to have those selfish desires fulfilled.

The Hebrew word for **delight** means, "to be soft or pliable." (See James Strong's *The Exhaustive Concordance of the Bible*, Nashville: Abingdon, 1890, "Hebrew and Chaldee Dictionary," #6026.) When a person *delights* himself in the Lord, he allows God to *reform* his heart, making it soft and pliable to *His* will and purpose.

If we truly delight ourselves in the Lord, then our will is

transformed, seeking His desire and not our own. When we completely delight ourselves in the Lord, our carnal desires will be replaced by His desires as our heart becomes united with His. Once our heart reaches that place of softness and submission, we learn to totally trust Him in every area of our lives.

Psalm 37:4 is speaking of a complete "heart transplant," in which we turn our will over to the Lord, seeking His will and trusting Him to lead us in the way He wants us to go. As our desire becomes His desire, we are promised that we shall have the godly desire of our heart.

Spiritual manipulators twist Scripture to give substance to their controlling prayers. They do not have the heart of God. Spiritual controllers think they know what is best for everyone involved. Because they do not have the *heart* of God, they cannot know the *will* of God.

Believers do not need to be concerned about controlling prayers if they are following the will of God, seasoning themselves in the Word, and developing godly character. You can prevail against any soulish prayers that hinder you. Practice the Word of God every day. Develop a sensitivity to the Holy Spirit. Commit to godly character and integrity. These principles produce security in Him and enable you to follow as He leads you.

SPIRITUAL WISDOM

Since we are spiritual beings, we are open to the entire spiritual realm of good and evil. Just because we sense something spiritually, does not mean it is from God. Every thought and desire must line up with the Word of God. If we think every thought comes from the Spirit of God, then we are seeing ourselves as infallible and are being misled.

The greatest need of the church is to know and understand the laws of the Spirit. Fully maturing our spirit man produces discipline and wisdom in our lives. The loss of spiritual wisdom can hurt the move of God. When we refuse to take the time to mature our own spirit man, revival will be short-lived.

CONTROL BY SPIRITUAL GIFTS

Unfortunately, some misuse their spiritual gifts to control others. We do not discount the gifts of God in any way, for they are priceless to the body of Christ. However, we must understand the character of God, so we can know when the gifts are in true operation. One of the attributes of the Holy Spirit is that He will always exalt Jesus — not another human being.

I have been in meetings in which the eyes of the people were called to focus on "the man of God" and how "he would heal" and "he would bring deliverance." It is a sad fact, but some people are ready to follow anyone or anything that appears "spiritual." Only God will heal and bring deliverance; and while it is true that He may use man to reveal Himself, He alone must receive all the glory, praise, and honor.

The flesh attempts to control the moves of God. Many things that people label "spiritual" actually come from the mental realm. You will know whether something is of God or not by discerning whether it points toward or away from self. If someone has a revelation or a prophecy that benefits, exalts, or glorifies self, then it is not of God.

Suppose you are in a church service where everyone is rejoicing, shouting, and praising God, when suddenly someone raises his hands and yells, "Thus saith the Lord." They then deliver a supposed prophecy. (Read 1 Corinthians 14 for a detailed study of the proper functioning of the gifts of the Spirit in public gatherings.)

After the person has given the prophecy, everyone in the meeting screams, "Yes!"

But your spirit says, "No!"

Do not be swayed by such "hyper-flesh" moves and prophecies. We must mature ourselves and hear the voice of the Lord accurately. We must not accept a prophecy as an operation of the Spirit just because the majority of the people seem to be ecstatic about it. Do not follow the *mood* of the people; follow the *move* of the Holy Spirit.

Many are mesmerized by spiritual gifts. They are so awed by an exciting display that they do not stop to discern what is true and what is false.

Wherefore by their fruits ye shall know them.

Not every one that saith unto me, Lord, Lord, shall enter into the kingdom of heaven; but he that doeth the will of my Father which is in heaven.

Matthew 7:20,21

Jesus taught that we will know the servants of God by their *fruits*, not by their *gifts*.

The security of the flesh is always centered in another person and their gifts — not in God. Security in God is motivated by commitment, rather than by control.

HAVING A RENEWED MIND

In true guidance from the Spirit of God, the human spirit and a renewed mind work together. The spirit gets the plan for the situation, and our mind agrees with the Word of God. The guidance is not impulsive, and our intelligence is not in constant rebellion to it.

When we receive instruction from the Holy Spirit, if our mind has been renewed in the Word, we will *submit*. Even if the mind does not understand, if it has been renewed, it will agree in faith with the plan the Holy Spirit has given. If we find ourselves in constant disagreement with the Holy Spirit, our common sense leaves us.

There are certain situations that call for a quick and seemingly impulsive response or action. These situations usually mean life or death, and the mind doesn't have the time to think. In these situations we operate from the prompting of the Holy Spirit. But in the long-range plan of God, the renewed mind must be in a *faith agreement* with the Holy Spirit.

When we shut our minds off altogether, we open ourselves to a driving spirit. When a person is "driven," they are not cooperating with God. They operate in the natural rather than the spiritual. A driven person is in a never-ending cycle. There is always something *urgent* that they need to deal with. Being in their presence is exhausting. Even their words weary you. They begin to look old and tired far ahead of their years.

Being driven is extremely dangerous. When a person is driven, they are under attack and portions of their life will not "add up" according to the Word of God. This is where deception enters in. They are hardened to human needs and desires, because they are works-oriented. As a result, they become a *taskmaster* and insinuate everyone is to follow that direction, or they are not following God. Ministry to people is not high on their list of priorities. This attack of the enemy is not only designed to destroy the driven individual, but countless others as well.

If you are in this area of attack, then get back to basics. Refuse to be driven. Refuse to let your fellowship with God be sidetracked. Refuse to let impulsive desires become action. Season yourself by the Word and under the authority of godly leadership.

WALKING IN THE SPIRIT

This I say then, Walk in the Spirit.

Galatians 5:16

If you commit yourself to walking in the Spirit, you will not be controlled by anyone but God. Any demonic spirit attacking you, either directly (trying to get you to be a controller) or indirectly (trying to control you through someone else) will immediately be exposed by the Spirit of God inside your spirit man. Then you can take authority over it in Jesus' name and get it out of your life.

When your mind is renewed by God's Word and you are walking in the Spirit, you will not be led astray by controlling powers.

CHAPTER 5

CONTROLLING POWERS OVER THE SOUL

The main problem of society going into the new millennium will not be the fear of war, the AIDS epidemic, or the homeless. It will be *mental illness*. There is a great struggle between the forces of darkness and the Holy Spirit for the soul of man. If the enemy can render us immobile through our mind, then our spirit cannot follow God.

Toothpaste and orange juice commercials used to corner the market. Now we continually see ads for help with mental problems. One television ad shows a nice looking young man lying on his bed at home. His parents walk in and scream, "Why can't you work? Why can't you get up and go to school? What's your problem, you lazy person?"

Then the announcer comes on and says, "He's not physically ill. He is mentally ill. If you are like this or know someone who is, call this toll-free number."

The soul of man has often been misunderstood by the church and is usually ignored. Scientifically, we can't pinpoint just exactly how the mind operates. However, God created the soul of man, and He meant for every part of our being to be used to its greatest potential.

There are five key areas to the human soul: the *will*, the *emotions*, the *intellect*, the *imagination*, and the *memory*. All five of these were created and designed to be used according to the Word of God. Each area of our soul is to be generated by our spirit. The Holy Spirit should inspire and influence our will, our emotions, our intellect, our imagination, and our memory.

Unless we understand how the enemy attacks our soul, the desire of God's Spirit will not manifest itself through us. When we have an unharnessed soul, our carnal desires will dominate our lives.

And be not conformed to this world: but be ye transformed by the renewing of your mind, that ye may prove what is that good, and acceptable, and perfect, will of God.
Romans 12:2

Although our spirit is secure the minute we are born again, we are to constantly renew our mind with the Word of God and stand against the attacks upon it. When an attack hits, the spirit man always bounces back faster than the soul. The soul must learn to renew and strengthen itself through the Word of God. Sitting under strong, anointed preaching helps to discipline our mind. Praise and worship also motivates the soul to pursue God and keep our mind focused on Him.

We have the ability to understand our will, emotions, intellect, imagination, and memory and mature each one. We *can* possess our whole man. If you are fighting a battle in your soul, *purpose* in your heart to win. Neutrality in any form spells defeat. We must determine in our mind to move forward before an outward manifestation can be seen. Internal security always produces outward stability.

ATTACK ON THE WILL

God created man with a will. He doesn't want robots to love and serve Him. He receives pleasure when we choose to serve Him.

It is our choice to serve God or the devil. It is our decision to give in to sin or live in righteousness. Even after we are born-again, it is our decision to experience the things of God or just dutifully go to church on Sunday. It is our decision to accept or reject the call to ministry.

The human will is sovereign. God will not violate it, but we can't make wrong decisions and then blame God for the outcome. Responsibility comes with the human will. He is not responsible for our choices — we are.

The human will is attacked by the enemy through passivity and lethargy. These words can be defined as "sluggishness, inactivity; drowsy dullness."

That is not what a Christian is supposed to be like. We are to be a people who are excited, courageous, creative, and enthusiastic. When the human will is under attack, we lose our zeal for God. We could care less if the Gospel is ever preached again. We become lazy, careless, and slothful. Our discipline and diligence are gone.

Indecisiveness becomes the predominant factor in our lives. We can't see or hear what is wrong or right. Instead of the godly strength to live by our decisions, we rely on the opinions of others. What another man says carries more weight than what we know in our hearts. If we continue like this, we will end up confused and doubting, tossed by everything we hear.

The enemy causes our will to become passive through constant vexation or harassment. We must understand that the enemy very rarely hits one time. Instead, he constantly, day in and day out, beats us until we are worn out. When he has beat our will to a thread and we have not renewed ourselves by the Word of God, then one more hit will knock us out. That's why we wake up one morning and find ourselves in sin. That's why we look around one day and find our marriage in shambles and our family falling apart. That's why some marry the wrong person. It's because their will was made weak through constant vexation.

The devil cannot violate our will. He must have our permission to take over. Even a nonbeliever has the willpower to say *no* to the devil.

The Holy Spirit will never override your human will. Instead He speaks to it, witnesses to it, and instructs it. But He will never violate it. The choice is yours.

If you are being pressed daily, harassed and tormented to fall into sin, then you are under a spiritual attack. The battle is over the control of your will. In order to win, you must begin to strengthen yourself through the Word of God. Find the scriptures that deal with the trouble you are facing. Let strength and encouragement from the Word give you the courage to stand. Look at the situation squarely in the face and speak the Word of God to it. The Word of God is designed to handle the pressure. Adverse circumstances melt at the spoken Word. No matter how weak your will seems today, through the power of the Holy Spirit, you can make it stronger.

Remember that eternal consequences are far greater than the temporary trials we face. The action of your will is eternal. Fight for what God has given you, and do not bow to the temporal onslaught against you. *The moment of trouble will pass, but the decisions you make will stand forever.*

THE WILL OF THE ENEMY

Just as we have a will, Satan himself has a will. God created him as Lucifer, a beautiful archangel, the chief musician who led worship in heaven. But through his will, he followed after pride and thought *he* would take over the throne of God. (See Isaiah 14:12-14.) As a result, he was kicked out of heaven like lightning. (See Luke 10:18.) Through a choice of his will, he perverted his own destiny and is forever cursed by his choice. He is now Satan, the enemy of God and man.

The goal of Satan is to steal your will for God. In doing so, he can eventually destroy you. When your will for God is gone, poverty, sickness, disease, calamity, and disaster come. Your joy and strength can be robbed from you through the lack of willpower. Passive decisions or indecision can even cause physical death.

THE WILL OF SAMSON

Samson was a man born of great physical strength. Before his birth, an angel appeared to his mother and said her son would deliver the Israelites from the enemy. This angel also told her the source of his strength, and what he must do in order to perform the will of God for his people. (See Judges 13.)

Samson had a wonderful childhood. The Spirit of the Lord came upon him many times during his youth. He once tore a lion apart with his bare hands, and he slew a thousand men with the jawbone of a donkey. But Samson had one problem, he loved the women of the world and chose them over the women of God.

Because Samson did not follow the Word of God for his life, he opened the door for the enemy to destroy him. Samson's strength was directly linked to his will. Had his will been submitted to God, he would have been invincible. He would have not only had physical strength, but the spiritual strength to say *no* when the enemy came. But through repeated sinful pleasures, his human will was weakened by a stronger human will — the will of Delilah.

Delilah was a Philistine, and the Philistines had kept the people of God in bondage for years. The only thing that stood between them and the Israelites was the strength of their leader, Samson.

No physical strength could capture Samson. No army had been able to contain him. So the Philistines approached Delilah and offered her money if Samson would tell her the secret of his strength. Three different times she begged Samson to tell her his secret. Although he tricked her those three times, his will was becoming weaker and weaker. Finally, the fourth time came.

And she said unto him, How canst thou say, I love thee, when thine heart is not with me? thou hast mocked me these three times, and hast not told me wherein thy great strength lieth.

And it came to pass, when she pressed him daily with

her words, and urged him, so that his soul was vexed unto death;

That he told her all his heart.

Judges 16:15-17

Samson's will was pressed and vexed until he succumbed. As a result, he was robbed of his strength and taken into captivity. In the end, as he cried out for the mercy of God, more Philistines were killed than ever before, but Samson died along with them. (See Judges 16:30.)

We must fight for and protect our will. As we deeply plant the Word of God into our will, the plan of God is easier to follow. With the Word as our substance, it is easier to stand against the schemes of the enemy. When controversy comes, when the enemy attempts to beat us down, we will have the strength to shout "No!" in the face of trouble.

For a time, it is possible to perform certain feats for God in our own physical strength, but they will not last. Only inward security produces lasting outward stability. When the spirit man is strong, the will latches on to it. As a result, the works we do for God will be lasting.

I've seen many strong men and women fall into the trap of relying on their own strength for the ministry. They get so caught up in the *works* of God, they fail to renew themselves and keep their spirit man strong. Sadly, the works they accomplish fall away and become a spectacle to believers and sinners alike. Like Samson, you cannot fight spiritual battles without the strength of God.

We are not to confuse the gifts of the Holy Spirit or the anointing with the strength of God. We may have an anointing from God to heal the sick, but that does not mean our will is linked with God's will. Do not confuse the two, because the gifts from God are another subject entirely. We have a responsibility to build up our inner man through the Word of God in spite of our accomplishments, great or small.

I have told this story before, but it is worth telling again. In my grandparents' day there was a minister greatly used in the gifts of God. He had such a powerful anointing that all he had to do was raise his hand and everyone in the prayer line would be slain in the Spirit. Many healings took place. Yet, he ran off with another woman.

It really bothered me that something like that could happen. What was the problem? He had a weak will. He had not taken the time to build his inner man and become strong. When the attack of the enemy came, he fell. He relied on his gift as his strength.

The gifts are "extra," my friend. Where the rubber meets the road is in whether or not your human will is merged with the will of God in every situation. The whole armor of God and the principles of the Word of God must be grafted into your own will.

God is requiring more from us as leaders and believers. Maturity and discernment must come forth from the body of Christ. God will require an answer for our accomplishments, whether they were lasting and accurate or weak and failing. Our goal should be a lasting accomplishment.

THE WILL OF JOSEPH

There is also a great lesson to be learned from a man named Joseph. Although Joseph made minor mistakes in the beginning, he learned from them and turned them into godly strength later in his life. Joseph had developed an inner strength that caused his will to remain strong and fixed with God's will.

Joseph had been sold into slavery to Potiphar, an Egyptian officer. But because the spirit man of Joseph was strong, God prospered him and brought great favor to him. Potiphar trusted him and promoted him as overseer of his entire household. (See Genesis 39:4.) However, the enemy had other plans.

And it came to pass after these things, that his master's wife cast her eyes upon Joseph; and she said, Lie with me.

But he refused, and said unto his master's wife, Behold,

my master wotteth not what is with me in the house, and he hath committed all that he hath to my hand;

There is none greater in this house than I; neither hath he kept back any thing from me but thee, because thou art his wife: how then can I do this great wickedness, and sin against God?

And it came to pass, as she spake to Joseph day by day, that he hearkened not unto her, to lie by her, or to be with her.

And it came to pass about this time, that Joseph went into the house to do his business; and there was none of the men of the house there within.

And she caught him by his garment, saying, Lie with me: and he left his garment in her hand, and fled, and got him out.

Genesis 39:7-12

The enemy will often wait until great favor and recognition come to us before he launches his greatest attack. If we are not prepared, we can fall into his schemes.

Joseph's will resisted the temptation, but one initial response doesn't shake the enemy. He continued to harass and torment Joseph through this woman, hoping to weaken his will and cause him to fall. Had Joseph's will not been fused with the will of God, this vexation would have caused him to fall. But Joseph was strong in the Lord and ran from the trouble. This was not a cowardly action, but rather he showed the enemy who was in control. Because his will was immersed in the will of God, he knew exactly what to do.

Part of learning to "run the race" is knowing when to run away and when to stay. There is a time to run, just as there are times to stay and confront. There were times when Paul confronted, and there were times he fled the city.

Potiphar's wife ended up falsely accusing Joseph, but the accusation could not stand forever. (See Genesis 39:16-23.) The enemy plagues us the best he can, but we'll always be victorious when our will is submitted to Him.

Had Joseph succumbed to the attack of the enemy, his destiny would have been thwarted. Our enemy works the same today.

POWER OF THE WILL

The human will has more power than the rest of the soul. Let's say you've just finished a huge meal and dessert is being brought to the table — your favorite chocolate cake.

Suddenly, your *imagination* rises up and you think, "I just know that creamy fudge icing is heaped an inch thick on that cake."

Your *memory* recalls, "Remember how rich and moist that cake is? Remember how great it tasted last Christmas?"

The *emotions* join in, "You know how much fun we have eating mom's chocolate cake together. We can laugh, and talk, and have a good time!"

Your *mind* begins to signal the rest of the body, your eyes focus on the cake, your mouth begins to water, your stomach is full but says, "I'll make room!" and out of nowhere the *will* steps in and shouts, "NO!"

That ends it right there. The rest of your soul and body rebels, but your will made a decision and that's the final word. Every other part of you has to line up to whatever the will says.

The same is true in the spirit realm. When the rest of our soul wants to get out of line, the will has the authority to bring us back on track. That's why it doesn't matter how you feel in order to gain a result. You will always feel either up or down, but the will is your mainstay. Your will always makes the final decision, right or wrong. Your will is the strongest part of your soulish being.

When our will is obedient to God, the rest of our soul soon follows. The human will is the disciplinary factor of the soul. The human will is not automatically born again like the spirit is. Our mind must be transformed by the Word and the unction within us to serve God and fulfill His purpose on earth.

The human will begins to function before birth. As a fetus inside the mother, the baby uses the will to move its arms and legs. Once born, it is the job of the parents to train the will of the child. When a child has a temper tantrum, they have an uncontrolled will that must be taught discipline and control.

When we are born again, our will changes. We now have a will to serve Him — to do what is right and pleasing to Him. From the moment we are saved, our will is submitted to the plan of God and ceases to be our own. From that day forward, it is intended for our will to be disciplined and trained by the Word of God, producing life, health, and joy, no matter what circumstances are surrounding us.

There is no greater joy than to merge the human will into the will of God. When the human will and the will of God become one, we are invincible. There is no foe that can stand, no attack that can conquer. There is no disease that can destroy and no curse that can come.

ATTACK ON THE EMOTIONS

Just as God has given us a will, He has also given us emotions. The emotional side of mankind is a world all its own. By nature, man's emotions are unruly. They are an unharnessed frontier that must be conquered by the spirit man. When they are led by the Holy Spirit, the door is open for the mercy of God to be manifested. Our emotions can show the joy of God, the grievance of the Spirit, or the urgency of the hour. The emotions can express the anger of the Lord or the peace He extends to the troubled mind.

Due to a lack of knowledge, many in the church are widely led by their emotions. Because of this error, many are taught that it is unscriptural to feel anything, or when they do, to lie about it and say they don't. But the fact is, we *do* feel things in our soul, good and bad. It is not wrong to have emotions, but we must control them and not let them control us. When decisions are made based on our emotions, our emotions are controlling us and we are out of balance.

We are not to use our emotions to manipulate or control another person. We are not to use them to find the will of God for our lives. We are not to use them to prove the Spirit of God is working in our lives. Our emotions are not the basis of true love or the lack of it.

However, just as color adds life to a black and white picture, so our emotions were created to do in our individual lives. Our emotions were not made to rule us, but to enhance us. They were made to show detail and depth. They were given to show the personality and heart of God. They were not created to be the sole expression of our being, neither were they created to remain dormant.

Just as the rest of our soul, our emotions must be matured through the Word of God. When we feel something contrary to God's Word, it is wrong. Emotions undisciplined by the Word of God have the potential to steal our destiny.

Our emotions come from two sources: the unregenerated man or the born-again, Spirit-filled man. When emotions come from the unregenerated man, they are carnal. They are in opposition to the Word of God, and they want to be in control. Because the world does not understand Spirit-led living, they operate entirely by their emotions and intellect.

Many become controlled by their own emotions, because they make their decisions primarily based on *feelings* — whatever feels good, do it! If they wake up one morning and do not *feel* a positive emotion for their mate, they leave them. If it *feels* good to have an illicit relationship, they do it. If they don't *feel* like showing up for work, they don't go. Their life is in constant confusion, because their emotions are always up or down. This is precisely why they make so many wrong decisions!

The emotions are the same in the believer, the only difference being that the spirit man has the final say in the matter, not the emotions. We can't afford to make decisions based on our feelings. If we are ruled by our emotions, we cannot stay in communion with God. Prayer is not answered on the basis of emotion. Prayer is answered when it is spoken in faith, according to God's Word.

Our emotional realm wants to rule our lives whether we are born-again or not. But when we have a personal relationship with Jesus Christ, He becomes the "rudder of our soul." When He guides us, our emotions line up to the Word. They are not allowed to "trick us" in things contrary to Scripture.

LIVING BY EMOTIONS

If we have not yet disciplined our emotions to submit to our spirit and the Word of God, we are open territory for the attacks of the enemy. When the enemy cannot gain entrance into our will, he heads for our emotions. If he can get our emotions to follow him, the attack weakens our will.

A sure sign of an emotional attack is in the area of self-pity. When self-pity rules us, our view becomes warped. We feel that everyone is against us and no one likes us. We begin to feel that everyone else is wrong and we are right.

Our first reaction is to withdraw from being under fire and run for protection. But when we withdraw, we pull the harness off of our emotions, allowing them to rule us. When self-pity becomes the basis from which we view everything, the enemy wreaks havoc within us.

Self-pity turns into arrogance, which is an area of pride. Arrogance is a protective device of the mind. Many who have been hurt wear arrogance as a covering to hide their wounds. When we wear that false cloak, we cut off the blessings of God into our lives. We are unable to hear His voice when He speaks. Even if we hear Him, we cannot break out of the sheath of arrogance to be obedient.

Another area where the enemy attacks our emotions is anger. When we have been hurt by another, our emotions pull to the forefront and anger is usually the first to surface.

When an animal is badly wounded, vultures follow it, circle it, and when the animal can no longer defend itself, they attack and eat their prey. These dumb and skimpy birds do nothing to cause the downfall of their prey, they just take advantage of their weakened condition.

In the same way, wounds in people attract evil spirits. Unless those hurts and wounds are dealt with, the enemy will follow us, circle us, and aggravate us until those hurts cause our downfall. If the wound is not dealt with, he will feed upon it until you are consumed. Many have left the ministry, left their mates, or left their calling because they did not recover from a hurt and became angry.

We cannot play with hurts and wounds and they won't go away if we ignore them. Hurts and wounds that have not been attended to are the primary reason why believers need deliverance. Although a believer cannot be possessed by a demon in their spirit, they can go through similar stages of oppression, depression, and obsession in their soul and body.

When anger dominates us, every action results in strife. Revenge becomes our utmost desire. We are only pleased if those who hurt us are hurt themselves. We feel the need to hurt whoever crosses our path. Anger will eat away at us like a cancer. It's never satisfied, and it eventually turns into deep bitterness. We will begin to look for negative support, then gossip and slander surface and we find ourselves in total confusion.

Instead of living in the righteousness, joy, and peace of our spirit, emotional anger produces a *wilderness*, causing us to feel isolated and alone. We no longer trust anyone and would rather live our life alone. When we allow the enemy to gain ground in our emotions, we act as carnal men. Our emotions are not equipped to see into the spirit realm, so we are only moved by what we see in the natural. If that is the case, the devil will make sure we see and hear a lot.

Jesus said unto him, Thou shalt love the Lord thy God with all thy heart, and with all thy soul, and with all thy mind.

Matthew 22:37

If the enemy has our soul preoccupied with our hurt and tormented by our problems, then we are not focused on God. Maintaining a clear and free soul by walking in forgiveness opens the door for the love of God in us. Then His purpose can be fulfilled through us.

ABUSIVE CONTROL OF EMOTIONS

There are those who will attempt to control us through the use of personal power and unnatural respect, which is *emotional manipulation*. Tears and helplessness, anger, threats, and silence are all instruments of emotional manipulation.

TEARS AND HELPLESSNESS

A classic example of emotional manipulation starts when both sets of parents want a newly married couple to spend the Christmas holidays with them.

It begins innocently enough when the bride mentions to her mother, "I think we are going to visit John's family for Christmas."

The mother starts crying and complaining, "You don't love us anymore, or you would come to our house for the holidays!"

This negative reaction throws the daughter into an emotional state. She wavers and finally agrees to change their plans.

But when the bridegroom calls his mother with the news, she is equally upset, "But we have everything all planned!" she wails. "We can't possibly change things now!"

Many people are controlled through such displays of emotions. Often, when someone doesn't agree with the controlling person, that person will whine, "You don't love me," or, "You don't want me around anymore." But not all abusive controllers rule with an iron hand. Some come clothed in sweetness and gentleness and are particularly dangerous. If they can't manifest a tear, they will revert to helplessness. Their intention is to make their victim feel an overwhelming sense of responsibility to them.

Such controllers know how to play on the strings of guilt and pity. They control through their supposed sickness, weakness, and victimization. Although their ailments or infirmities are sometimes legitimate, more often they are fabricated or exaggerated. They make their victims feel that if they are not pampered and petted, their whole world will crumble.

If you find yourself being exploited by this type of abusive control, be gentle but firm. Let that person know that you are not going to allow yourself to be emotionally manipulated.

If someone tries to make you feel obligated to change your established plans just to suit their selfish desires, do not give in to them. If you are being abused by a sympathy-seeking exploiter, you may have to be blunt with them. Let them know you will not be manipulated.

Don't fall into the trap of emotional manipulation by thinking that something is wrong with you. Judge yourself by the Word of God. If you have peace within, then know that the emotional outburst of the other person is an indication of their *problem* and not a reflection on you.

ANGER

If a display of tears and helplessness won't work, often a controlling person will resort to anger — and most people do not know how to handle an angry person. Stay calm. Do not overreact, as an entire chain of negative events could be set off. Don't do anything that might provoke or justify improper behavior. Sometimes it is good to leave an angry person alone with their rage. By refusing to react to anger, you diffuse the power of this type of abusive control.

Anger will monopolize the atmosphere as well as your thoughts if you are not careful. Angry words will hit your mind like machine-gun bullets, preventing you from defending yourself properly. Keep your perspective clear and precise.

THREATS

Words of failure, defeat, guilt, criticism, and intimidation are all threats used to control a person's life. They are designed to paralyze with fear.

> **Death and life are in the power of the tongue: and they that love it shall eat the fruit thereof.**
>
> **Proverbs 18:21**

> **The words of his mouth were smoother than cream or butter, but war was in his heart; his words were softer than oil, yet they were drawn swords.**
>
> **Psalm 55:21 AMP**

> **Behold, they belch out [insults] with their mouth; swords [of sarcasm, ridicule, slander and lies] are in their lips; for who, they think, hears us?**
>
> **Psalm 59:7 AMP**

Just as a sword or an arrow pierces the heart in a battle, so negative words are designed to pierce the heart of the hearer. If words are spoken negatively and abusively, they will wound and hurt deeply. No one can carry negative words in their heart and still fulfill the plan and purpose of God for their life, just as they cannot walk around with a sword or an arrow thrust in their chest!

Words of failure and defeat dominate the lives of many people without their even being aware of it. Pull these negative, abusive words out of your heart by counterattacking them with the Word of God.

> **For the Word that God speaks is alive and full of power — making it active, operative, energizing and effective; it is sharper than any two-edged sword.**
>
> **Hebrews 4:12 AMP**

Speak the Word of God over yourself. It will calm and heal the wounds of abusive words. Negative words can affect your life only if you allow them to do so.

SILENCE

Silence, which is a form of rejection, is an especially powerful emotional tool. If tears, anger, and threats don't work, the controlling person will use silence as a weapon. They shut out their victim by ignoring them and keeping them dangling, wondering what the controller is thinking and how they are feeling. Weak people are easily controlled because they cannot handle such treatment.

If someone is trying to control you through silence, let that individual be silent! Go on with your business and your life. Don't get into turmoil because of what someone else is or isn't doing. Make a choice to live in joy and contentment.

EMOTIONAL FREEDOM

How can we break free from emotional control? By forcing our emotions to be silent, trusting the Word of God, and maturing the spirit man — no matter what is happening around us. Although we cannot see these attacks with our natural eyes, the consequences are very real.

The Psalms are a great disciplinary book for the soul. Amidst trouble and calamity, David forced his emotions to be subjected to the Word of God.

O Lord, open thou my lips: and my mouth shall shew forth thy praise.

Psalm 51:15

Make me to hear joy and gladness.

Psalm 51:8

I trust in the mercy of God for ever and ever.

Psalm 52:8

I will hear what God the Lord will speak: for he will speak peace unto his people.

Psalm 85:8

Why art thou cast down, O my soul? and why art thou

disquieted within me? hope thou in God: for I shall yet
praise him for the help of his countenance.

Psalm 42:5

Once I understood the spiritual implication of emotional attacks,
the Psalms became a source of strength for me. The words of David
became alive as never before. In all the above verses, David took control of his emotions. It didn't matter who was right or wrong. What
mattered was how David himself dealt with the situation. David had
enough wisdom to know the trouble would pass. He could take his
experience and live in bitterness or move on into greater wisdom and
strength. We can see from his life that he chose the latter.

The situation you face today may be much the same. We all face
emotional attacks, but we must allow the Holy Spirit to rule and
reign over our emotions. Look to the Psalms when under attack.
Begin to express them with your own cry to God. Before long, your
emotions will silence themselves, your spirit will take supremacy, and
you will no longer be moved by what you see. The enemy will have
no doorway to your emotions if you seal them with the Word of God.

UNDERSTANDING OUR INTELLECT

The human brain is extraordinary. No scientist or medical doctor
is able to explain how this small mass of tissue can retain and understand knowledge. Human intelligence is unexplainable by science,
because God created it to function in His image.

However, our human intelligence can be an enemy to the works
of God. Intelligence is a wonderful thing and should be sought after,
but the world has made it their "god" and used it as their sole source
of survival.

The world's intelligence places mankind in "class categories." It
does not see all men as equal. If someone doesn't think the way "our
class" does, then they are considered uncivilized or barbarian. But
God sees men according to their *heart*, not their *intellect*.

Intelligence was placed inside of man to help him understand the workings of God and cause prosperity to abound in the earth. Combined with the Spirit of God and the Word of God, intelligence accomplishes great feats. No matter what culture we are in, if we prosper in that environment, intelligence serves us. For example, I doubt a city businessman could survive in the wilderness for very long. Yet, the people who lived in the wilds, outside of an office building, are labeled "incompetent." The world has widely misused their definition of intelligence.

GODLY INTELLIGENCE

God desires to reveal Himself to us and have us know His ways. He intended for intelligence to work with our spirit to cause understanding.

Come now, and let us reason together, saith the Lord: though your sins be as scarlet, they shall be as white as snow; though they be red like crimson, they shall be as wool.

Isaiah 1:18

God delights in using our intelligence to understand His ways. The Hebrew word for **reason** means, "to decide, convict." (See *Strong's Concordance*, #3198.) Our intelligence has a part to play in conviction and submission to God. Only a fool says, **There is no God** (Psalm 14:1).

We should not seek after intelligence, but after wisdom. Only God can give us wisdom.

For the Lord giveth wisdom: out of his mouth cometh knowledge and understanding.

He layeth up sound wisdom for the righteous: he is a buckler to them that walk uprightly.

Proverbs 2:6,7

The fear of the Lord is the beginning of knowledge: but fools despise wisdom and instruction.

Proverbs 1:7

He that getteth wisdom loveth his own soul: he that keepeth understanding shall find good.

Proverbs 19:8

Happy is the man that findeth wisdom, and the man that getteth understanding.

Proverbs 3:13

Wisdom is the principal thing; therefore get wisdom: and with all thy getting get understanding.

Exalt her, and she shall promote thee: she shall bring thee to honour, when thou dost embrace her.

Proverbs 4:7,8

From life's experiences, intelligence will turn into godly wisdom if we discipline our soul according to the Word of God. Godly wisdom produces peace and security. It is a safeguard from destruction and poverty.

NATURAL INTELLIGENCE

Natural intelligence, or intellectualism, is resistant to God, because it wants to rule in His place. Natural intelligence thinks it is wiser than God and sets up rules and regulations to prove it. The theory of evolution was born from an intelligent mind. It reasoned our existence far less than what it really is and came up with its own source. I would say it is much easier to believe in a Supreme Being rather than happenstance.

Natural intelligence has to figure everything out. It is logical to the point of disregarding anything supernatural. There are no miracles to the natural intellect. By solely relying on the natural intellect, one cannot see the purposes of God. The gospels aren't logical — they are spiritual. Intelligence must remain submitted to the reality of God if it is to be of any use.

On the other hand, many have set up religious rules and regulations for multitudes to follow. They reason that you cannot serve

God unless you do certain things on certain days. The Pharisees and Sadducees were good examples of intelligent men who reasoned their service to God by works alone. There was no worship or service from the heart. If an act was done contrary to tradition, such as a miracle, it upset their intelligence and they rejected it.

Although natural intelligence has accomplished tremendous feats, it cannot be the only source we draw knowledge or truth from. Our spirit man is to be the prime function of our being, and our intelligence is to follow the leading of our spirit.

ATTACK ON THE INTELLIGENCE

The goal of the enemy is to dethrone God from His rightful position in our life, using tricks and deception to accomplish this goal.

How can we tell when our intelligence is being attacked? First and foremost, logic overrides our inward witness. Our faith and belief in God begin to fade. Sadly, most cults of the world started from a leader who was attacked in his mind and didn't recognize it.

We may be living our life as usual, but the thoughts come, "God isn't real. There is no such thing as healing or deliverance." We begin to intellectualize everything we see. The only things that motivate us are success-oriented exhortations that stimulate our intelligence. The enemy has us thinking we are superior and objective, but we are playing the fool.

Before long, we feel cold and dead inside. We don't want to pray. We objectively criticize the Word of God. We certainly will not tolerate the preaching of the Gospel, and we find ourselves opposing everything we hear from the pulpit. If we don't fight this attack, we will begin to look at the local church as a bunch of weak, dependent, low-life people who need a crutch to get through life.

COMMON SENSE UNDER ATTACK

Along with our intellect, the enemy attacks our common sense. If the devil cannot get you to question the existence of God, he'll try to throw you into the land of no common sense.

I once heard a preacher say, "Why is it when some people get born again, they seem to throw out their common sense?"

God expects us to use our common sense, fine-tuned by the promises of His Word and the unction of the Holy Spirit. For example, there are those who will confess healing scriptures all day, then they'll go outside in sub-zero weather without a coat. They don't take care of themselves, but expect the blessings of God in their bodies. Then there are those who constantly claim prosperity for themselves but never look for a job. Yes, it is true that God provides for the sparrow, but even she leaves the nest to get the worm!

Do not lose your common sense. Do not take important details for granted. The Word of God is not a "cure-all" when you have not done your part. The principles of God are not magic. They are principles of faith, and faith means some action on your part. Faith, together with inspired action, overcomes any obstacle in your path.

But wilt thou know, O vain man, that faith without works is dead?

James 2:20

UNDERSTANDING OUR IMAGINATION

The imagination is a very spiritual part of our soul. It is one of our most valuable assets. We have the ability to imagine far beyond our intelligence. For example, we can imagine something and still not intelligently put it together. We might envision a goal or a dream and still not have the intelligence to know how to accomplish that goal or fulfill that dream.

Imagination without action in its proper timing is fruitless. It is heartbreaking to hear the godly imagination of a person, then watch them sit and do nothing to fulfill it. Ten years later the person has the same vision — maybe greater — and still isn't working towards their goal. I love a person who has imagined a dream and then takes steps to see it happen.

Our imagination has the creative ability to do anything for God.

It can build creations that humanity has not yet seen. Imagination is a powerful force with the ability to change nations, cities, churches, and communities.

If we do not understand how the imagination works, we will dream our life away. Faith is not fantasy. Idle imaginations cannot produce anything, physically or spiritually. But if you see something in your imagination that is inspired by the Holy Spirit and lines up with God's Word, it is within your reach.

I was aware of the call of God on my life as a young boy. I would read my Bible, pray, and shut myself in my room. I had a huge map of the world on the wall. I would stand in front of it and preach to it. I would point my finger to different places and say, "I'm coming to you!"

That was my godly imagination, envisioning the plan of God for my life. But I didn't stop there. That map of the world isn't paper hanging on my wall; it is now the ground of nations I walk on.

Our imagination is unlimited and comes from a desire in our heart. It works when we are daring enough to believe it and will stop at nothing to see it work. Our ability has nothing to do with our intelligence, which is often a hindrance to our imagination. Our ability stems from a godly imagination and a willingness to see what we have imagined accomplished.

IMAGINATION OF DAVID

David used his imagination when he slew Goliath. When he went out to face the giant, he envisioned in his head what would happen. Goliath attempted to intimidate him, but David's vision was stronger than the giant's words.

And the Philistine said to David, Come to me, and I will give thy flesh unto the fowls of the air, and to the beasts of the field.

Then said David to the Philistine, Thou comest to me with a sword, and with a spear, and with a shield: but I

come to thee in the name of the Lord of hosts, the God of the armies of Israel, who thou hast defied.

This day will the Lord deliver thee into mine hand; and I will smite thee, and take thine head from thee; and I will give the carcases of the host of the Philistines this day unto the fowls of the air, and to the wild beasts of the earth; that all the earth may know that there is a God in Israel.

And all this assembly shall know that the Lord saveth not with sword and spear: for the battle is the Lord's, and he will give you into our hands.

1 Samuel 17:44-47

David imagined it, put it into action, and it happened.

GODLY IMAGINATION

When a heart is submitted to the plan of God, all of the imaginations are an overflow from the Spirit of God. The plans we envision further the kingdom of God and turn the hearts of man towards heaven. There is no self-exaltation in godly imagination. True imagination, inspired by the Spirit of God, is humbling, knowing it is something we can never attain without the strength and wisdom of God.

Casting down imaginations, and every high thing that exalteth itself against the knowledge of God, and bringing into captivity every thought to the obedience of Christ.

2 Corinthians 10:5

Imaginations that exalt themselves above the Word of God are not from heaven. If the enemy cannot get us to imagine selfish dreams, he will try to turn those godly thoughts into self-exalting imaginations. You must guard against those attacks and seek to bring God glory in everything you do.

A WORLD OF FANTASY

In this troubled generation, multitudes are searching for a way to escape the pressures. The entertainment world offers a variety of creative fantasies. As a result, young people are mimicking acts of violence and perversion they see in movies and hear in music. They are unable to draw the line between reality and fantasy. They do not face the real issues of life. One day they wake up and find their life has gone nowhere. They are so grieved and mentally depressed, they commit suicide or bring harm to others. These same people may have everything going for them, but they allowed their imagination — their mind — to be manipulated by the devil.

And they shall turn away their ears from the truth, and shall be turned unto fables.

2 Timothy 4:4

For we have not followed cunningly devised fables, when we made known unto you the power and coming of our Lord Jesus Christ, but were eyewitnesses of his majesty.

2 Peter 1:16

Neither give heed to fables and endless genealogies, which minister questions, rather than godly edifying which is in faith: so do.

1 Timothy 1:4

The Bible warns us concerning the excess of fantasy and fables. An unhealthy exposure to fantasy can cause you to lose your purpose. If you have been hurt, wounded, or are under attack, the enemy will tempt you to indulge in fantasy as a way of escape. Fantasy causes your imagination to become passive. If your imagination is passive and empty, be sure that something will come to fill it. If your mind is filled with the whispers of the enemy, you will end up following them. Don't be misled by the enemy and think it is harmless. *A world of fantasy is very dangerous.*

The Word of God does not say that having fun is wrong. God invented fun! He is a God of joy. But turning away from the truth towards fantasy, following fantasy, or giving heed to fantasy — especially when you are hurting — opens the door for the enemy to confuse you and destroy you.

You will guard him and keep him in perfect and constant peace whose mind [both its inclination and its character] is stayed on You, because he commits himself to You, leans on You and hopes confidently in You.

Isaiah 26:3 AMP

Be aware of the schemes of the enemy. Keep your heart humble before the Lord. Discipline your imaginations by the Word of God. God wants you to have a creative imagination. Do not let it go in the wrong direction. Line every imagination up with the Word of God and ask yourself, *"Is God exalted, or am I?"*

ATTACK ON THE MEMORY

The human memory is fascinating! Every scene we visually see, every thought we have, every word spoken to us, everything we read, and everything we eat is automatically stored in our memory.

The memory is so valuable that when a person loses it through injury or disease, they no longer know *who* they are. They can no longer recognize sights that were once familiar to them. Although they still have a will, an intellect, an imagination, and emotions, they have lost their identity as a person, because they have lost their memory.

If the enemy can harass and torment your memory, he can *paralyze* you. It's that simple. When we have been seriously hurt from an attack of the enemy, it sears our memory. If we do not deal with these hurtful memories and effectively recover from them, they will have a crippling and disastrous effect on our personality.

That is a terrible way to live. Why should we base our lives on the hurts and wounds of the past? Our *future* is not based on the hurts of the *past*. Everyone has been hurt and wounded at one time or another, but we are to stand on the promises of God and allow the Holy Spirit to minister healing to us. God has a great and wonderful future planned for us.

"For I know the plans I have for you," declares the Lord, "plans to prosper you and not to harm you, plans to give you a hope and a future."

Jeremiah 29:11 NIV

The devil tries to use our memory as an art gallery of pain. He will cause familiar, painful circumstances to surround you and say, "Remember how that hurt you? Let me walk you through the gallery of your hurts. See that hurt? Remember this painful experience?" If we listen to his voice, we will succumb to fear.

Fear causes withdrawal and paranoia. If the enemy has access to our memory, everyone we meet will be sized up according to our hurts. We are afraid to trust anyone. How can we walk in unity if we remain an island to ourselves? How can we walk in the confidence of God if we mistrust all those called to help us? We cannot hide in fear very long. It is like a poison inside of us, destroying the work of God.

Fear is the force Satan operates through, just as faith is the power that moves heaven into the earth. Fear robs us of the faith of God. As faith produces life, health, and peace; fear produces death, disease, and torment.

Fear robs us of a good conscience. Maybe you did something wrong. Maybe you gave in to carnal sin. Even though you have repented and according to 1 John 1:9 you were forgiven, the enemy will attempt to rob you through your memory. When you go to pray for the sick, he will remind you of a sin, as though it was not forgiven. If you submit that memory to Satan, you will feel unworthy to be used by God and will be rendered useless for His kingdom.

A tormented mind produces hate and hardness. It operates in impulsiveness, trying to escape the bad memory. It suspects evil in every person. It covers itself in a false pride. Because it operates out of fear instead of faith, it has lost hope and cannot help others in trouble.

If we operate like this for very long, we will lose the soundness of our mind. Mental wards are filled with hopeless people who never recovered from emotional hurts and wounds. Medical science goes to great extremes to administrate peace to patients, but medication will not heal the hurt; it can only offer a temporary reprieve.

GODLY MEMORY

And Saul said to David, Thou art not able to go against this Philistine to fight with him: for thou art but a youth, and he a man of war from his youth.

And David said unto Saul, Thy servant kept his father's sheep, and there came a lion, and a bear, and took a lamb out of the flock:

And I went out after him, and smote him, and delivered it out of his mouth: and when he arose against me, I caught him by his beard, and smote him, and slew him.

Thy servant slew both the lion and the bear: and this uncircumcised Philistine shall be as one of them, seeing he hath defied the armies of the living God.

David said moreover, The Lord that delivered me out of the paw of the lion, and out of the paw of the bear, he will deliver me out of the hand of this Philistine. And Saul said unto David, Go, and the Lord be with thee.

1 Samuel 17:33-37

David used his memory to give him the courage to believe God for deliverance. He remembered how God had been with him in past trouble, and because of those great victories, he knew God would be with him in this feat as well. His memory ignited his faith, and he conquered the giant without fear.

Our memory was designed to bring into remembrance the good things the Lord has done for us — the times of salvation, healing, and deliverance. Our memory can bring an unflinching trust in the plan of God, not because of who we are, but because of His great faithfulness.

Notwithstanding the Lord stood with me, and strengthened me; that by me the preaching might be fully known, and that all the Gentiles might hear: and I was delivered out of the mouth of the lion.

And the Lord shall deliver me from every evil work, and will preserve me unto his heavenly kingdom: to whom be glory for ever and ever.

2 Timothy 4:17,18

Paul also relied on his memory to give him courage to fulfill his God-given mission. He knew that if God delivered him from evil before, He would do it again.

Don't let the enemy steal from your memory. Keep your mind stirred up, remembering often what God has brought you through, how He has provided for you, and the times He delivered you.

We must protect our memory by the Word of God. If God tells us repeatedly to remember His Word, then we know the plan of the enemy is for us to forget it. Begin to condemn what is condemning you. Reverse its effect and verbally condemn the torment. Command the tormenting spirits to leave your memory. Purpose to forgive those who have hurt you. Look past the hurt to the faithfulness of God.

If it is memories of sin that are harassing you, fight back with Scripture.

If we confess our sins, he is faithful and just to forgive us our sins, and to cleanse us from all unrighteousness.

1 John 1:9

As far as the east is from the west, so far hath he removed our transgressions from us.

Psalm 103:12

Maybe you have been paralyzed by fearful stories and events. Pregnant women are especially prone to this attack, as so-called friends have a vast array of horror stories to tell of pregnancy and childbirth experiences. Perhaps the enemy has led you to believe that you will experience the same outcome. Fight back! Do not allow the devil to rob you of your destiny through fear. When David was afraid of his future due to stories of the past, he said:

Deliver me, O Lord, from mine enemies: I flee unto thee to hide me.

Teach me to do thy will; for thou art my God: thy Spirit is good; lead me into the land of uprightness.

Psalm 143:9,10

Whatever situation you face, God's Word has the answer. The future is what I call "virgin territory." No man has yet walked into it. The future is bright and does not have to be tainted by what we have already lived through.

Remember ye not the former things, neither consider the things of old.

Behold, I will do a new thing; now it shall spring forth; shall ye not know it? I will even make a way in the wilderness, and rivers in the desert.

Isaiah 43:18,19

But this one thing I do, forgetting those things which are behind, and reaching forth unto those things which are before,

I press toward the mark for the prize of the high calling of God in Christ Jesus.

Philippians 3:13,14

Paul recognized the power of his memory, good and bad. He made a statement here in verse 14 that spoke loudly to his soul. No matter what else he accomplished, his first priority was to "forget the things that lay behind him" and press on into the future.

We must set our face like a flint and refuse to subject ourselves to the past. Strength and power will come to you. You have authority over your memory. You choose the thoughts you meditate on. You were sent to the earth for a purpose. Do not lose it from a careless memory. Gird up the loins of your mind, and conquer the ground placed before you!

VICTORY IN OUR SOUL

Our first step in breaking evil control over our soul is to repent. We must ask the Spirit of God to make Himself real to us and show us how our will was swayed, our emotions began to rule, our intellect became exalted, our imagination turned destructive, or our memory was captured by the enemy.

Ask Him to soften your hardened heart and give you new eyes and new ears to see and hear His Word and the voice of His Spirit. Force yourself to be at church service. It doesn't matter if you want to go or not — *be there*! God will see your faithfulness and meet you there! One day, you will walk into the service out of a true desire to worship Him rather than a duty.

Purpose to be vulnerable to the message from the pulpit. Ask God to show you how it applies to your life. Begin to tithe and support the work of God.

Get involved in the outreaches of your church. Ministry to others always seems to put things in perspective. Be friendly and reach out to others in fellowship.

Command the spirit of unbelief to leave you in Jesus' name. Take authority over the harassing, tormenting spirits sent to vex your thoughts.

Fellowship with those who are strong in the Lord and seek after godly wisdom. Those who walk in godly strength will not condemn your temporary weakness. They will exhort you and live a victorious life in front of you. They will sharpen you as you gain strength and be a balance for you.

Submit your will, your emotions, your intellect, your imagination, and your memory to the discipline of the Holy Spirit and God's Word. You do not have to fall subject to the enemy through pride, unforgiveness, or a hardened heart. You can recognize any attack against you and defeat it before it gains any hold on you.

You are valuable to God and His plan so let your soul express the character and personality of God, just as it was designed to do.

CHAPTER 6

CONTROLLING POWERS OVER THE BODY

Thou art worthy, O Lord, to receive glory and honour and power: for thou hast created all things, and for thy pleasure they are and were created.

Revelation 4:11

We were created to bring God pleasure, even in our bodies. Our body houses our spirit man. Through our human body our spirit man is able to fulfill the will of God. If our body dies, the spirit leaves. That is why the human body is also a prime target of the enemy. We think of bodily attacks as something that affects our physical body only, but when we are in pain or discomfort, it is more difficult and sometimes impossible to do what God has called us to do.

The human body — our natural flesh, tissues, blood, membranes, organs, and nervous system — was created as an individual. No one is created exactly like another.

The carnal man idolizes the human body, looking only at the flesh and not understanding who the "real" man is. Although we recognize one another by human form, that is not the *real* person. That is our shell, or what I call our *bodysuit*. The real person is the spirit man. The spirit man is eternal and lives forever. The body that so many idolize will eventually die. When we get to heaven, we won't recognize one another by body form, but by our spirits.

Our body is a vessel by which the Holy Spirit speaks and moves, the Gospel is carried into the nations, and the works of God are seen. He works through us to heal the afflictions of another and to minister to the lost. He chooses to speak His oracles through our mouth.

And Stephen, full of faith and power, did great wonders and miracles among the people.

And they were not able to resist the wisdom and the spirit by which he spake.

Acts 6:8,10

The human vessel has always been important in the plan of God. Stephen yielded himself to the Spirit of the Lord to preach the Gospel. The religious leaders of the day had resisted the influence of the Holy Spirit up to that point. But with Stephen being **full of faith and power**, they could no longer resist the message of Jesus Christ.

Jesus wants to live through our human body to show His strength and compassion to the world. His desire is for the Scriptures to come alive through our mortal flesh.

ATTACK ON THE HUMAN BODY

The human body houses five different senses: sight, smell, sound, touch, and taste. If these senses aren't disciplined, the devil will tempt us by appealing to them.

Television, billboards, magazines, films, and other materials stimulate the senses of our human body. We must be careful about what we gaze upon and what we listen to. When the flesh yields to these distractions, we cannot please God. We must guard our senses from all evil, as they are the entrance to our body.

But he was wounded for our transgressions, he was bruised for our iniquities: the chastisement of our peace was upon him; and with his stripes we are healed.

Isaiah 53:5

Jesus paid for the afflictions of our body. Not only did He take the sins of the world with Him to the cross, He also took all diseases and sicknesses of the body. He shed His blood, paid for them, and pronounced healing for all who would believe Him.

Sickness and disease are attacks of the enemy on our body. The devil wants to hinder our labor for the Lord and destroy our flesh. He does not want the power of God revealed through us. If he cannot destroy our soul, he will attempt to devastate our flesh.

Jesus hates sickness and disease because it destroys our bodies. He is not intimidated by it, nor does it influence His power. Jesus commissioned us to preach the Gospel and to heal the sick and all manner of disease. (See Mark 16:15-18.) A large portion of Jesus' ministry was healing the sick. He does not want the human body to suffer. If the body is suffering, how can we effectively minister the Gospel to the lost?

Verily, verily, I say unto you, He that believeth on me, the works that I do shall he do also; and greater works than these shall he do; because I go unto my Father.

John 14:12

Know that you have been given authority and power over every evil thing. Jesus didn't *ask* the spirits of infirmity to leave people's bodies, He *commanded* them to leave. He used His authority over every sickness, and we have been given that same authority.

Do not give place to these attacks. Stand against them, and call them what they are. Many times, the spirit of fear keeps these symptoms working in you. I have talked with many people plagued by migraine headaches. One person said that each time one came, they checked themselves to see if they feared something. When the fear was discovered, they rebuked it and the pain left immediately.

Wherefore take unto you the whole armour of God, that ye may be able to withstand in the evil day, and having done all, to stand.

Ephesians 6:13

If you need a physical healing from actual disease in your body, keep believing the Word of God. Listen to anointed preaching of the Word that professes and believes in the healing power of God. Read testimonies of healings. Build up your faith to receive God's best. If you don't see healing as you think it should come, continue to stand. Do not let Satan get the victory!

One other area we need to guard in order to stay healthy is simply operating in good judgment and temperance in the natural. For example, don't let the devil torment your time of rest. Calm your thoughts and speak peace to them.

I will both lay me down in peace, and sleep: for thou, Lord, only makest me dwell in safety.

Psalm 4:8

If the enemy can rob our rest, he can gain entrance into our soul. Many people have fallen into sin simply due to a lack of rest.

We must take care of the physical man through good eating habits, exercise, and rest. If we are physically tired, overeat, or never get any exercise, it is hard to gain spiritual strength. If we do not take care of our physical bodies, our time on the earth can be cut short. Many people die early, in spite of medical technology, because they neglect their physical bodies.

God desires that we give our bodies to Him as a living sacrifice. (See Romans 12:1.) This isn't a dead, lifeless sacrifice, but a living, healthy one. He wants to live through our bodies and show the world His love and power.

According to my earnest expectation and my hope, that

in nothing I shall be ashamed, but that with all boldness, as always, so now also Christ shall be magnified in my body, whether it be by life, or by death.

Philippians 1:20

Becoming dead to your flesh does not mean life ceases to be exciting. Allowing Christ to live through your human body is the most thrilling experience on earth! Do not allow the enemy to cheat you from experiencing all that God has for you.

Take care of yourself, guard your senses, and stand against any attack of sickness with a vengeance. You will find it is a lot easier to serve God and allow Him to use you for great exploits when you are strong in body as well as spirit!

CHAPTER 7
WHO'S IN CONTROL?

Controlling spirits most often attempt to work through the people nearest us, such as family members or very close friends. Many times, the person being controlled doesn't even realize it because it is simply a way of life for them. It may be the *only* way of life they have ever known.

Parents can consciously or unconsciously limit a young person's ability to succeed in life. This happens because of negative, fearful, or even unscriptural family attitudes or customs. We must be careful that the normal control in a family situation — such as the natural control the Bible indicates a parent is to exercise over a child — does not become abusive.

Neither give heed to fables and endless genealogies, which minister questions, rather than godly edifying which is in faith: so do.

1 Timothy 1:4

The Greek word for **genealogies** is partially derived from a root word used to refer to "something said, reasoning, or motive." (See *Strong's Concordance*, #1076.)

Endless genealogies can be limitations inherited from family members or handed down through family philosophy and tradition.

Many times a response or reaction comes from a motive shadowed by spirits of poverty, fear, or bitterness. These motivating spirits will bring about abusive control. We must break these controlling spirits and nullify their effects upon us.

Some responses of those motivated by such controlling spirits may sound like the following:

• "No one in this family will ever buy a new car, only a used one."

• "No one in this family will ever leave our church or denomination, because our grandfather helped establish it."

• "No one in this family will marry without the approval of the other family members; no one is allowed to follow their own heart in these matters."

Every family has its weak points, no matter how spiritual they may seem in other areas. There is no such thing as a *perfect* family. But endless genealogies often become controlling factors in the way people live and train their children. Christian couples should not rear their children this way. Believers need to break away from these ungodly hindrances and limitations and train their children in the victory and likeness of Christ!

Training our children is our responsibility and our commitment to them. It means living godly lives in front of them, teaching them, and directing their lives by word and example. Training does not smother, overprotect, or control out of fear. Leave room for children to experience joy outside of parental authority.

Depending on their age and maturity level, let your children learn to make certain decisions on their own. Sure, they will definitely make mistakes, but these are controlled mistakes. Making small mistakes now and learning from them will prevent tragic mistakes down the road.

For example, if you have given your ten-year-old a list of household chores to do, don't stand there breathing down his neck until those chores are accomplished. Instead, give him a time frame to complete them. If they are not completed at the specified time, special privileges are lost, such as watching a special television program or spending the night with a friend. It's your child's choice — do the task or suffer the consequences. This teaches them responsibility beginning on a small scale. As they grow older and more is required of them, they learn to accept and fulfill their responsibilities. The end result is a mature, responsible adult, trained in the ways of the Lord.

RELEASING CONTROL

To every thing there is a season, and a time to every purpose under the heaven.

Ecclesiastes 3:1

There is a proper time for everything under the sun. When children grow up and choose a life partner, it is time for parents to let go of them and respect their marriage. Perhaps nothing has controlled you, but rather you have been the controlling one. Maybe you didn't even realize it. Realize it now! It's time to let go.

When parents refuse to release their married children, it causes major problems. They visit the newlyweds and tell them what they should or should not do, and walls of division go up. When grandchildren are born and the grandparents start telling the parents how to rear their children, there is even more strife and tension.

When a couple asks their parents or in-laws for advice, it should be given. But unless their advice is sought, parents should keep quiet and pray! Unfortunately, some parents can't wait to be consulted — they just barge in and tell their children how to live.

Parental interference causes friction in marriages. Some marriages never survive this interference and are unable to break their parents' control over their lives. Unfortunately, some divorces are actually a result of interfering parents!

I am not saying that every in-law is a potential problem-maker, but in-laws who attempt to control their children do cause problems. The most prevalent in-law problem is found in controlling parents who won't release their daughter or son. Such people have no trust in their own training of their children.

When a parent's sense of security and self-worth is vested in their son or daughter rather than in their relationship with the Lord, problems arise. When the child is out on their own, the parents realize their source of security, which is the child, is now gone — and they don't know what to do. They are no longer around their child all the time to monitor and control their actions. These parents can live in such insecurity that they go into a frenzy!

Parents, if your children are married, release them to God. Look at the situation realistically. When you and your mate were first married, you had to find out how to live and make it together as a family. You made some good choices and some bad choices. You had rocky roads and smooth roads. You spent money wisely and sometimes foolishly. When the romance seemed to leave the marriage, you stayed together because of a commitment. You had to discover *together* how to build a strong family. You survived, grew, and matured — so will they.

Give your children the freedom to discover life with their mates on their own. If they come to you for advice, give it. But after it is given, leave them alone. If you have trained your children by the Word of God, then you are not their foundation — God is, and you should rest in that fact.

Look at this time in your life as a fresh, new beginning for you and your spouse. It is never too late to develop security in God and to begin a new adventure in life. It will take work if much of your married life has centered around your children, but you can do it. Begin by asking your children to forgive you for interfering or not letting go. Then ask the Holy Spirit to show you how to pray for your children's marriages and be a support to them. The days ahead can be the best ones of your life if you will make the right decision today to *love, let go,* and *live.*

ABUSIVE CONTROL BY SPOUSES

Some husbands who have no spiritual balance in their lives turn their wives into weary, battered "nobodies." It is not exciting to live with a "doormat." Most of these women were not that way when their husbands first met them, but they relinquished their individuality because their mates were always misusing the scripture: **Wives, submit yourselves unto your own husbands, as unto the Lord** (Ephesians 5:22). The constant demands and the abusive control they endured for so long finally wore them down to a point of bare existence.

There is a true, biblical attitude of submission on the part of a wife toward her husband. That kind of submission is of God, but it is nothing like that which is demanded by a selfish, overbearing companion. Wives are to submit to their husbands, but not to the point of disobedience to the Lord.

Ephesians 5:25 goes on to instruct the husbands: **Husbands, love your wives, even as Christ also loved the church, and gave himself for it.** Christ loved the church so much that He died for it. Husband, are you willing to die for your wife? A godly husband does not make unloving *demands* on his wife. Let the character of God be your character towards your wife or your husband.

I have met many women who cannot do anything unless their husbands first approve of it. They live in constant fear of making their mates angry. Such women are limited by only the things their husbands allow them to do, or the places he allows them to go. All these women can say is, "Whatever you want, dear."

That's not being submissive — that's being a robot! This kind of dependent relationship is smothering and unnatural. It is based on insecurity and is in danger of destruction. Too much dependency will drive a person away. No one can protect their position and security by being overly dependent. We were made to express life and to fulfill the purpose of our Creator in the earth. Anything that hinders that will eventually self-destruct.

Abusive control and domination cause the loss of human dignity. In such a marriage, the controlled partner doesn't become a "help mate," they become a "slave mate." That is not God's plan for marriage. An overbearing husband destroys the life of his wife and children. An overbearing wife destroys the life of her husband and children.

Some of these hurt and wounded wives become involved in the feminist movement as a protective or defensive mechanism. Some join because they need to feel like they are in control of *something*. On the other hand, some women are just as selfish and self-centered as these insensitive men.

I once met a pastor's wife who did nothing but consume soft drinks and watch soap operas. She would not cook breakfast for her children, help them get off to school, or make any effort to clean the house. She didn't believe that any of these tasks were her job.

Controllers try to act like God, because they are out to serve their own selfish needs and desires. They are never considerate of others. In their eyes they are so wonderful and so right. They think everyone loves them, because everyone serves them.

However, when there is love in a marriage, there should be mutual consideration. There is no question of "whose job is this?" and "whose job is that?" The partners aren't selfish; they help each other.

Remember this — God is our Source and Comfort in every area of life. Every prospering relationship stems from that revelation inside of us.

PORTRAIT OF A CONTROL VICTIM

Several years ago, I was ministering in a church where I met a woman who was a perfect example of a control victim.

Before the evening service, I was sitting at my book table in the back of the church when I watched this woman enter the building. She was pushing three rowdy children ahead of her like a flock of geese, and they were all under five years of age. They were toddlers with all the energy and abandon of their age, doing everything at once — screaming, hollering, laughing, and crying — the whole works. It takes two parents even to attempt to corral this many young dynamos, and this woman was trying to do it all alone.

Then I saw the door shut behind a man who had a mean look on his face. What I saw shocked me. I thought to myself, *Something is wrong with this man. Maybe he's oppressed.*

The woman really had her hands full, so I walked down the aisle and helped her take off the children's coats. She didn't know I was the visiting preacher.

"I wonder where my husband is," she said with a strained look on her face. "Oh, there he is!"

Guess who the husband was? The man who had walked through the door and caused my spirit to sound off like an alarm: "There's something wrong...something wrong...something wrong!"

The man had already found a seat. He didn't even stand up to help his family enter the row. He just pulled back his knees so they could squeeze through. In the process, one youngster escaped and began running down the aisles. I picked him up and plopped him in his father's lap, saying, "Here's your child."

As I did so, I noticed that neither the wife nor the children were dressed very well, but that the man was wearing a nice suit.

That night I preached a sermon on control, and to be perfectly honest, I directed it right at this man. Afterwards, the woman came up to the front of the church and stood in the prayer line. As I laid hands on her and began to pray for her, I felt a reaction in her husband, even though he was still in the congregation, and I withdrew my hands from her.

We've got a big one here tonight! I thought. *This is a major controlling spirit.*

So I laid my hands on the woman's head again, and this time I was determined not to budge. I knew she wanted to be free.

"I need your help," she whispered to me. "You're the first preacher who has let me know what I'm in. I thought my husband and I were living the way we were supposed to, but then I saw that other people's marriages were not like ours."

This woman wasn't talking about material things. She was referring to the normal interaction between husband and wife — loving each other, holding hands, taking care of the children together, and enjoying life with one another. That's what people get married for!

As I was praying for her, the Holy Spirit began to do a work in her. Her face started to glow, but then something struck her soul with a shock! It was her husband's controlling spirit reacting.

"Don't get upset," I told her. "Just let the Holy Spirit do His work. God wants you to be free."

It was almost half an hour before she was completely set free. She was finally able to see her value as a person. With the Word of God and scriptural counseling from their church, this couple's marriage was eventually made whole.

The leaders in that church should have dealt with that problem years earlier. We are brothers and sisters in Christ, and when there is a situation among us as bad as this one, the church elders and deacons should help the pastor confront it and restore liberty and peace to those affected.

If you are forced to deal with a situation like this one, don't advertise the fact — just do it! The controlling husband or wife may react violently at first (any evil spirit will "blow up" when confronted directly), but deal with the problem with love and firmness — in the power of the Holy Spirit.

FINANCIAL CONTROL

Just as control works most often through the *people* closest to the victim, so it also works through the *thing* closest to the one being controlled. The saying is true: "If God has your heart, He has your money." We must be sure that we direct our money; we must not allow money to direct us.

There is another saying: "He who pays the piper calls the tune."

There is a great deal of truth to this quote as well. A number of people will try to control you through money during your lifetime.

It started when you were a child. Your parents exerted a certain amount of control over your behavior through your allowance. You were probably expected to perform certain tasks around the house or in the yard in exchange for your allowance.

Later in life, your bosses exerted a great deal of control over your behavior and job performance through your salary. These kinds of control through money are normal, as long as they are not excessive in any way.

Parents — especially wealthy parents — tend to use money as a means to control their adult children. Spouses also use money as a lever of control — especially when both partners work.

Unfortunately, many churches have prominent members who attempt to control with their money. They think that if they give large tithes and offerings, they have a right to issue orders. If everyone doesn't do exactly as they desire, they are not at all pleased.

If the pastor so much as preaches two minutes past twelve noon, they may threaten to reduce or withhold their offerings. If the pastor is not strong and his security is in money, he may quickly knuckle under to this type of financial pressure and agree to do anything demanded of him — without praying first or discussing the situation with the Lord — just to keep that large donation coming in! Such a pastor is depending upon flesh rather than on God.

Money is not head of the church — Jesus Christ is the Head of the church. These people need to learn that money is not given to the church to purchase power and prestige. Money is given to God as an expression of love.

The giving of money to God should be an established way of life for the believer. It is one means of sowing into the kingdom of God. We give so the work of the ministry can be fulfilled, lives will be changed, and miracles will take place. We worship God with our tithes and offerings, knowing that **it is he that giveth thee power**

to get wealth (Deuteronomy 8:18). He gives us strength to move and a brain to think creatively, so we can work and provide for our family. God is not limited, nor is He a taskmaster when it comes to giving.

Another controlling influence along these lines is *debt*. Being in debt means that you are, to some extent, under the control of other people. Debt can restrict the joy and achievement level of people's lives, and the pressure of debt can wreck marriages.

We must be careful not to let debt consume us. Debt is a "sneaky" hindrance. It can creep upon us and ruin our lives if we are not wise to it. Satan can use this means to bind the church and hinder us from supporting and giving to the work of the Lord around the world. We must be on our guard against this evil, because we are to finance the Gospel in the earth.

Give, and it shall be given unto you; good measure, pressed down, and shaken together, and running over, shall men give into your bosom. For with the same measure that ye mete withal it shall be measured to you again.
Luke 6:38

Bring ye all the tithes into the storehouse, that there may be meat in mine house, and prove me now herewith, saith the Lord of hosts, if I will not open you the windows of heaven, and pour you out a blessing, that there shall not be room enough to receive it.
Malachi 3:10

Whether the economy is strong or weak, we must operate totally by God's laws of giving and receiving. Be wise in your financial and business dealings, so you and your family can enjoy life on God's beautiful earth without the restraints of overwhelming debt.

One particular couple got in such terrible debt, they were unable to tithe and continue living on a daily basis. They couldn't let even one bill go unpaid without destroying their future. So the Holy Spirit instructed them to begin tithing toward the tithe!

They so desperately wanted to restore themselves in the area of giving that they began to tithe a small percentage toward what their normal tithe would be. They sowed seeds toward their financial restoration! As a result, today they give to their church over and above the required amount.

Money and debt do not have to control you. There is always a way, through the Holy Spirit, to gain back control over your finances. Then, when you see how God blesses you, you will grow in faith and prosper in all areas of your life.

CONTROL HINDERS THE FLOW OF THE SPIRIT

One principle in which God carefully trained me in the beginning of my ministry was not to depend on people's giving to pay my ministry expenses.

A frequent problem in the modern church is the fact that some preachers are dependent upon people's giving. They get so controlled by money that they lose the real flow of the Spirit!

This is one reason why some congregations are not moving on with God. A few people with controlling spirits are running things in the church, and the pastor doesn't want to lose them, because they are so influential in the city. However, their control, if not changed, will stop the move of God in that church!

By allowing people to control a church through their finances, we are looking to natural means as our provision. Jehovah Jireh is God, our Provider. Why look to man, whose means are limited, when we can look to God Almighty, whose provision is unlimited?

If you are a minister who is being controlled by someone in your church with money, hand the money back and say to them, "Here's your money. God is my Source. Unless your motive in giving is to serve the Lord and His church, please go someplace else where you can do what you want."

That person will most likely leave. He may even take some of the congregation with him. Let him go! The Lord will bring you more people with a heart after Him and a heart for service. You've just made room for them.

I had an interesting experience with one of these controlling types once. I had just preached about removing proud members of the church board and said, "If a deacon or an elder cannot flow with the Spirit of God, then he should be removed from the board."

A man offered me money if I would get up and retract what I had said.

I replied, "I won't retract what I said, because it was right. But you can give me the money anyway."

He didn't and I found out later that he was the problem in the church! This man wanted me to retract my statement because my anointed words had convicted him of his sin. He wanted to see if he could manipulate me.

Sometimes people come up to me after a service, complaining, and wanting me to withdraw something I have said. If I am wrong about something, I will apologize. If I have said something that is not right, I will retract the statement. However, I will not withdraw from the anointing, and I will not apologize for being right.

If you apologize for something you said while under the anointing, it weakens your anointing and power. It causes you to falter in your stand and strength. The truth is the truth. When you stand with the truth, you will be right with God and right with the people.

Overall, to break free and stay free of controlling spirits, ask yourself — not just once, but every moment of every day, "Who is controlling me?" There is only one right answer — Jesus. If your eyes are focused on anyone or anything else, if your heart finds security and comfort in anyone or anything else, or if you are obeying anyone else, then you are headed for trouble.

Only Jesus can lead you in the right way and bless you beyond your wildest dreams. Today, make certain your trust for all your needs and dreams is in Him and Him alone.

CHAPTER 8
ENABLING ADVERSITY

Controlling powers are Satan's tool to render us ineffective for the kingdom of God. Breaking free from them enables the Holy Spirit to have control over us, so we can **walk worthy of God, who hath called you unto his kingdom and glory** (1 Thessalonians 2:12).

But what if you suspect that *you* may have a controlling personality? Perhaps you have realized for the first time that there are areas in your own life controlled by demonic forces or by another person. You want to experience God's freedom, but nothing seems to work. Or maybe you experience a *temporary* freedom, but it never lasts long.

Most likely, you are attracting these controlling spirits. This is not to say you are demon-possessed! But if you are enabling these spirits to operate in your life because of certain weaknesses you have, you are like a magnet to them. This is where our renewed spirit man takes over and gets rid of these evil spirits forever.

It is important for you to recognize whether you have a tendency to be an abusive controller or the one being controlled. Let's take a more in-depth look at the characteristics of an abusive controller.

• Abusive controllers think the only way they can be important or accepted is by giving orders and making demands.

Do not allow ambition and desire for power to "drive" you. Ambition and power-seeking will not produce godly authority.

The centurion answered and said, Lord, I am not worthy that thou shouldest come under my roof: but speak the word only, and my servant shall be healed.

For I am a man under authority, having soldiers under me: and I say to this man, Go, and he goeth; and to another, Come, and he cometh; and to my servant, Do this, and he doeth it.

When Jesus heard it, he marvelled, and said to them that followed, Verily I say unto you, I have not found so great faith, no, not in Israel.

Matthew 8:8-10

Jesus marveled at the centurion's humility. This military leader had learned the principle of godly leadership and authority. In his humility to those in authority over him, he had become an authority himself. He was a trusted leader, one whose commands were followed and fulfilled.

Humble yourselves — feeling very insignificant — in the presence of the Lord, and He will exalt you. — He will lift you up and make your lives significant.

James 4:10 AMP

When we are humble towards God, He will promote us in due season. When that season comes, our sense of worth will come from a trust in Him, not from our ability to give orders or commands.

• Abusive controllers feel possessive about a person or persons. They want others to "check in" with them because they know more than anyone else does. They never accept someone else's judgment of what they think they should do. They often belittle others because they are convinced others don't know anything.

Possessive people always try to make others feel totally ignorant and immature, that the only way they are going to survive is by consulting with the controller and doing what they say.

When anyone voices an opinion, they cut that individual down by saying, "Oh, that isn't true. You're wrong." They don't allow differing opinions or ideas to be discussed, accepted, or even expressed. The other person's voice goes in one ear and out the other while they continue to do their own thing. This is a very selfish attitude.

Always being right or always having the last word can be very irritating to those around you. It is possible that there are those who know more than you. You cannot find your security in always being *right*. Take the time to listen to what others have to say — you just might learn something!

• Abusive controllers feel intense jealousy over another person, which dictates their opinions and actions.

For example, if the person they have been controlling starts talking to someone else, they will automatically feel jealous, possessive, and threatened. They even go to the point of intruding in on the conversation in order to monitor it.

Love endures long and is patient and kind; love never is envious nor boils over with jealousy; is not boastful or vainglorious, does not display itself haughtily.

1 Corinthians 13:4 AMP

There is no room in a believer's life for this type of jealousy. Usually, it is best to sever this relationship if you are being controlled by their jealousy and even confronting them in love has not helped.

• Abusive controllers are threatened by another person's new relationships.

They are scared of losing your friendship. Therefore, if you speak to someone else, pray with another individual, go out to dinner with another friend, or engage in any other activity with anyone but them, they feel threatened.

This discussion is limited to people in friendship relationships, not to people in marriages. A married person's best friend should be his or her mate. A married couple is committed to each other in the sight of God and man. A certain amount of exclusiveness is an implied part of marriage.

Remember, *commitment* isn't *control*. Take a look at your friendships. Do you pout if your friends sit with someone else at church or in a school meeting? Do you give them the silent treatment if they make a new friend? If so, you are wanting to control them, and you are only harming your own friendship with them.

• Abusive controllers feel they must protect others from every experience life has to offer.

By shielding a person from life's experiences, you are guilty of carrying their responsibilities. Every individual must be accountable for his own behavior. Instead, a controller attempts to shield another from personal responsibility, then turns around and gets angry with the other person for not being more responsible. The controller then feels used, cheated, and abused.

This kind of overprotection can happen in any relationship, especially between a parent and child. When an individual has reached maturity, protecting them from life's experiences is *destructive* and doesn't help them in any way. The Bible says that godly wisdom and understanding come from God's Word and life's experiences. (See Proverbs 3:13 AMP.)

Experiences, both good and bad, groom our character and cause us to walk in the wisdom of God. The varied experiences of life, coupled with the Word of God, season us and bring us understanding.

Those shielded from life are not able to develop God's character or grow in His wisdom. This type of protection never ends, because with each one of life's experiences we go through, we are better equipped to handle the *next* thing that comes along.

We can't "fix" people's feelings, do their thinking for them, or solve their problems. We can love them with a genuine love, **with brotherly love; in honour preferring one another** (Romans 12:10).

An unnatural drive to take responsibility for someone else is actually an insult to the other person. The abusive controller is stating that the other individual is incompetent and incapable of making a choice or decision for themselves.

In such cases, usually the other person has never asked the controller for help. That is why the controller gets angry when the other person goes on their way, seemingly ungrateful.

Most abusive controllers truly believe they are helping others when they shield them from experiences. They think it is cruel or heartless to let others face up to their own dilemmas. They even twist and control the Scriptures on love and giving, but the Word of God should set us free — not hold us in bondage.

Do you look to others for your protection? Are you fearful of what each new day will bring? Each of us must go through our own experiences in life, but we are not helpless! Jesus Christ has given us a gift — the Holy Spirit living inside of us. We are to rely on the power of His Spirit within us to guide us and direct us in every situation. Man cannot begin to give us the divine wisdom we need for everyday living!

• A controlling person thinks and talks about the other individual all the time. If anything keeps the other person from spending time with the controller, the controller will attack that thing and attempt to get rid of it as quickly as possible. They will go to any length or any expense to make sure the person they are controlling spends the majority of their time with them.

This is *domination*, and it is not of God.

The controlling person will go so far as to dominate the other individual's vacations, dates, marriage, job, home-buying, church-going, or even personal finances if allowed to do so. If the other person is not careful, they can become so entwined with a controller that it can take years to get free of that relationship.

> **But seek ye first the kingdom of God, and his righteousness; and all these things shall be added unto you.**
> **Matthew 6:33**

Beware of seeking other people's advice for every decision you make. It is not wrong to seek wise counsel for major decisions, such as a job or the purchase of a home. But your vacations, personal finances, and church membership are things *you* are to control.

• An abusive controller reacts in an unnatural way to statements made about the person they are controlling.

For example, if someone makes a positive statement about the person being controlled, they will automatically criticize the controlled person to make sure that no friendship develops between them. On the other hand, if someone makes a negative statement about the controller, they will immediately defend themselves with a positive statement to make them look good.

Derogatory comments towards others are often used by the abusive controller, because it makes them feel superior. Take a good look at those who seem to be your friends when you are around, but you never know what they'll say behind your back. Just exactly what kind of friends are they?

Are you quick to make negative comments about others, or do you speak words of kindness?

Let all bitterness, and wrath, and anger, and clamour, and evil speaking, be put away from you, with all malice:

And be ye kind one to another, tenderhearted, forgiving one another, even as God for Christ's sake hath forgiven you.

Ephesians 4:31,32

• Abusive controllers attempt to overprotect — even to the point of hindering God's Spirit.

This type of control is often found in the local church. Sometimes elders or deacons can be so protective that they hinder the pastor from flowing under the anointing of the Lord. They don't help him fulfill the vision God has given him for that particular church.

Individually, an abusive controller can be so protective of another person that they will not allow that individual to venture out and experience God for themselves. They are afraid that the person being controlled will make a mistake; therefore, fear is the motivation for every decision.

We must learn to trust in the Lord in *all* things. If God has a calling on someone's life, He will give that person plenty of protection without help from us!

• An abusive controller makes plans for the other person without their permission.

If the individual being controlled doesn't want to follow the plan, they are usually made to feel so guilty that they end up going along with it anyway. They know that if they don't, all hell will break loose!

Has a relative ever volunteered your services on a certain project without your permission? You knew that if you didn't agree, there would be war in the family for weeks. That is abusive control.

God did not design human beings to live a miserable life under someone else's control, following someone else's plans and designs for their lives. His plans for us are greater than anything man could ever come up with. Don't allow others to make plans for you. Those plans may be the very thing that hinders you from experiencing the fullness of God. Look to Him for what tomorrow brings.

The steps of a good man are ordered by the Lord.
Psalm 37:23

• An abusive controller thinks the person they control owes them something and demands that it be paid back.

As an example, a mom and dad have a very good son who feels a call to the ministry, but because he enters Bible school instead of engineering school, his parents have a fit! They want him to have "security" in life and get a "real" degree.

They nag, cry, interfere, and generally do everything they can to get their son to change his mind, leave Bible school, and enroll at the local state university. (They also want him to live at home, so they can supervise him.) They stress that he *owes* them this consideration, because they are his parents and have devoted their lives to rearing him.

This is a perfect example of *control* versus *calling*. Such people fail to see that the call of God on an individual's life is the highest calling in life! There is a way to biblically "honor" one's parents and still go on with God. He is the One who must be answered to. The son should follow Elisha's advice — respectfully kiss his parents good-bye and follow God. (See 1 Kings 19:20,21.) The Lord will take care of the rest.

Trust in the Lord with all thine heart; and lean not unto thine own understanding.

In all thy ways acknowledge him, and he shall direct thy paths.

Proverbs 3:5,6

Do you trust God with your own life? Can you trust God with your loved ones' lives? If we do our best to be obedient to the call of God upon our lives, everything else will eventually fall into place.

• Abusive controllers try to manipulate through use of flattery.

Those who do not recognize God as their sole source and security will fall victim to flattery.

A lying tongue hateth those that are afflicted by it; and a flattering mouth worketh ruin.

Proverbs 26:28

To his neighbor each one speaks words without use or worth or truth; with flattering lips and a double heart [deceitfully] they speak.

Psalm 12:2 AMP

But as we were allowed of God to be put in trust with the gospel, even so we speak; not as pleasing men, but God, which trieth our hearts.

For neither at any time used we flattering words, as ye know, nor a cloak of covetousness; God is witness.

1 Thessalonians 2:4,5

Other types of controlling spirits can enter in through flattery.

The controller "pumps them up" by telling them how much he loves them, how wonderful they are, and what great things they have to offer — such as money. Then control through money becomes part of the game.

Our words are extremely powerful — speaking either life or death. A controller can also go to the extreme in the negative direction, offending and degrading others. They will cut others down with their harsh words in an effort to manipulate them. They have no regard for other people and their feelings. They are unable to see that God created all of us equally — in His image — and He is no respecter of persons. (See Acts 10:34.)

For we all often stumble and fall and offend in many things. And if any one does not offend in speech — never says the wrong things — he is a fully developed character and a perfect man, able to control his whole body and to curb his entire nature.

James 3:2 AMP

BUT GOD...

There is one more thing to be said about an abusive controller — they can all be turned around and changed for the glory of God. God can and does miraculously change people! We must not hesitate to go before the Lord, repent of controlling and being controlled, and ask Him to be in full control from this point on. He will empower us with His strength when we give every part of our lives over to Him and trust Him. As a result, our covenant with God regarding the plan and destiny for our lives can be fulfilled.

Faithful is he that calleth you, who also will do it.

1 Thessalonians 5:24

That is why we give ourselves to God. "Self" cannot be our source or our comfort. We cannot fulfill the plan of God on our own. That is why we say, "It is not some of self and some of God — *it is none of self and all of God."*

CHAPTER 9
RECEIVING VICTORY

There is freedom for those who are bound by control. Whether you have been the controller or the person being controlled, you *can* be set free!

If you are being controlled by someone else, here are some steps you can take to free yourself from that situation.

RECOGNIZE THAT YOU ARE BEING CONTROLLED

In the previous chapter, we discussed specific ways you can tell if you are being controlled. But in general, when you are around the controlling individual, you are not yourself — you feel intimidated and grow increasingly ill at ease around them. You wish your relationship were as happy and free as others you see.

You feel insecure and inadequate when you try to do new things on your own. Your hopes can be totally dashed and your mind thrown into confusion and instability if the other person makes even one negative statement.

You feel obligated to spend time with the other person, even though they have no consideration for your schedule or lifestyle. When you go out on a pleasant outing with friends or acquaintances, the controlling person, because they were not invited, feels threatened.

When you are pulled between two opinions, yours and the other person's, you feel obligated to agree with them. You lose your dignity to the point that you become careless about your appearance and lose your desire to be successful in life. You look and feel listless and exhausted.

Recognize how you are being controlled. Ask yourself, "Is their control through fear, guilt, obligation, anger, tears, frustration, confusion, or any of the other things we have discussed?" Whatever it is, find it, and exercise your God-given authority over it. Counterattack with the Word of God.

Do not respond to their efforts to control you. If you are controlled through silence, don't feel guilty when the controller doesn't speak to you for days on end. Go on and enjoy life. Let the other person be miserable if that is what they choose. Sooner or later the controller will realize that silence can no longer be an effective method to control you.

Often a husband will refuse to speak to his wife, or vice versa, because of something she said that he didn't agree with. He uses this childish weapon to punish her, instead of discussing the problem like an adult and resolving the issue. Two people cannot live in peace and harmony with this kind of strife going on between them. Disharmony hinders the movement of the Spirit of God.

The Holy Spirit will not flow through a clogged pipe! When you are grieved and hurt, the Holy Spirit cannot speak or work through you. In order to accurately hear His voice, you must be free from the hurts and bondages that come in life.

A controller may try to dominate you through words of inadequacy or failure, such as, "You can't do that. You'll fail because you're not educated." Many people thought that Albert Einstein was mentally retarded as a child. Abraham Lincoln suffered nothing but defeats and setbacks for years before he became a successful statesman. In fact, many of the most successful people in life never earned an academic degree. So don't let your past history of failures or your lack of formal education keep you from becoming all God intends for you.

A controller may even use threats against you, such as, "If you don't do what I say, I'm going to leave you!" Don't be intimidated by such negative remarks. Remember that the Greater One lives in you, and you are important to God. Attack those evil spirits by reminding them of who you are in Christ Jesus.

Then saith Jesus unto him, Get thee hence, Satan: for it is written, Thou shalt worship the Lord thy God, and him only shalt thou serve.

Matthew 4:10

Do as Jesus did — quote the Word of God to yourself and your adversary.

Control equals idolatry. Idolatry is anything that is placed above God. When a person does what someone else recommends instead of praying and seeking the Lord's direction, that is idolatry. When a person who is controlled becomes secure only in a relationship with his or her controller, it is a form of idolatry. Because both individuals in that relationship look to each other as their security, they become one another's god.

BREAKING AWAY FROM CONTROL

First comes the initial break from the controlling person. After you are strong in your spirit and know that your heart is right, you can take the next step in your complete deliverance from control — breaking ties! This usually means confronting the person who has exercised these controlling powers over you.

Confrontation does not always have to be a battle. But when confronting a controller, you must be strong. Controllers are not the most logical people to deal with. They have been blinded by their own insecurities.

You must say to them, "You have controlled me in these ways

(name them). These things will not work in my life anymore. You must change or we can no longer have a relationship."

When you do this, several things are likely to happen. As soon as you accuse the other person of controlling you, they will probably protest, "I'm not trying to control you. I love you. Everything I have done has been for your benefit. Do you mean to tell me that you don't appreciate it?"

Or the controller will turn the tables on you and try to hide their wrongdoing by making it appear that everything has been your fault. If you are not strong, you will slip from your stand and easily fall back into the clutches of control again.

The controller will continue, "You know I love you. We just have to work this out."

You will burst into tears and say, "Oh, I know." Then you are right back where you started.

The controller may exhibit all sorts of strong emotions all at once — anger, jealousy, pride, fear, and many others. Keep in mind that no normal human being could change emotions so quickly. This is further evidence of the controlling spirits at work within that individual.

Know that you are in a war, not on a vacation. If you are weak, you had better call on some strong prayer warriors to back you in intercession as you enter this battle.

After the confrontation is over, don't sit and meditate about what has happened. Shut it out of your mind. Instead of dwelling on it and rehashing it over and over again, get up and take a walk, praying as you go.

A PRICE TO PAY

There are always those who are not willing to pay the price to go on with the Lord. They would rather stay in their own little rut and not be concerned with change. If you truly desire to go on with God, you may have to make the very difficult decision to turn loose of friends or other close associates.

You will continue to pray for them, but may have to break all ties in order to maintain complete victory. Even a casual relationship with them can hinder you or dissuade you from fulfilling your godly call and purpose.

Do not bow to or serve the insecurities in another person. Do not allow fear to abort your destiny. Be bold and be strong. Walk in the compassion of God and take the nations in His name!

When you break the controlling power over your life, those controlling spirits will storm out of your life, and you will be left sitting all alone. You will most likely experience a certain degree of loneliness. You will also be struck with a feeling of guilt, followed by fear that you are not capable of making it on your own.

You may ask yourself, "What am I going to do now?" Don't panic, and don't give up.

Stop in your tracks and say, "Devil, move in Jesus' name! I break your power over me. Get off of me. You are a liar!" You have the authority to do this.

Then, when you are no longer under guilt or fear, you still must be on your guard. When you get up in the morning, make sure that you tell those controlling spirits to leave you alone. Break their power over you by commanding them to go from you, in Jesus' name. Quote scriptures to them and make them obey you.

Control is not just a psychological problem; it is also a *spiritual* problem. As we noted earlier, human nature is naturally controlling, but when control becomes unnatural, it is demonic and you must fight it in the spirit with God's Word.

The next time you meet the controller, they may not speak to you because you haven't been in contact or asked for help. But don't dare feel guilty or try to make up. You have just won your freedom, so enjoy it!

IT'S FINALLY OVER – OR IS IT?

Be strong and of a good courage; be not afraid, neither

be thou dismayed: for the Lord thy God is with thee whithersoever thou goest.

Joshua 1:9

When you have been in a spiritual war, you've stood, and you've won, you still need time to *recover*. Sometimes we shout "Hallelujah! It's over!" and think we can run the race at the same pace as before.

Don't be fooled by this attitude. Many who have successfully come through an attack fall during recovery, because they don't understand that it takes *time* to build strength again. They continue fighting something that isn't there, thinking they are still in the midst of a battle. Finally, they become worn out, discouraged, and give up.

Just as your body needs to recover from a physical illness, it must also recover from a spiritual attack. After the initial sickness is gone from you, and you begin to feel better, you can't run a marathon yet! The sickness is gone, the battle is over, but your body needs time to regain strength. The same is true in the spiritual realm. Don't rush yourself. Let God have time to work for you. Give yourself room to grow and mature in the things you have been through.

Remember not to overestimate or underestimate the war you have gone through. It is commendable that you made it. Give God the credit and use the wisdom He has produced in you.

Encouragement aids in your recovery and healing. Allow yourself to be the son or daughter of God, and let Him be the Father to you. It's good to hear Him talk to you and point out what the two of you did together. Rejoice with Him.

Remember these other basic points of recovery:

1. Pray in Tongues.

But you, beloved, build yourselves up [founded] on your most holy faith — make progress, rise like an edifice higher and higher — praying in the Holy Spirit.

Jude 20 AMP

This paints a picture of what faith mixed with praying in tongues can accomplish. An *edifice* is a structure. *Webster's Dictionary* defines it as "a large or splendid building." *Your faith, kindled by the Word and praying in tongues, causes you to rise and solidify yourself into a mighty, towering force.* No wind of doctrine or controversy can shake you with this combination. When we build ourselves up by prayer and the Word, our house will stand when trouble comes. Our fervent prayer will avail much. (See James 5:16.)

2. Sit Under Good Teaching.

Feed on the Word — the bread of life. When you are recovering, the Word of God is like cool streams of water to your whole man. Understanding and revelation come when the preaching is clear, sharp, and anointed. Read and devour the Word of God. It will strengthen and feed you, making you strong and unconquerable.

3. Worship God in the Privacy of Your Devotional Time.

This is not the time to be silent. Lift your hands, open your mouth, and praise the Lord! Dance before Him and receive the joy of His strength into your being. When you worship in spirit and truth, it enables you to walk above your circumstances. Join yourself with the congregation of the saints and pierce the heavenlies with praise and worship.

Praise him with the sound of the trumpet: praise him with the psaltery and harp.

Praise him with the timbrel and dance: praise him with stringed instruments and organs.

Praise him upon the loud cymbals: praise him upon the high sounding cymbals.

Let every thing that hath breath praise the Lord. Praise ye the Lord.

Psalm 150:3-6

4. Confess the Word.

Find scriptures that speak directly to your heart for this time of your life. Many scriptures have been listed throughout this book for you to use. They are life unto you. Allow them to transform your thinking. The Word of God is your armor. It promises to complete the mission it was sent to do, it will never return void or incomplete, and it will prosper in the areas spoken to. (See Isaiah 55:11.)

5. Have Someone Pray With You.

Your most trusted, spiritual friend knows how to pray for you. Their prayers can add to your recovery. Deuteronomy 32:20 says that one can put a thousand to flight, two can put ten thousand away. Why do alone what two together can accomplish?

Again I say unto you, That if two of you shall agree on earth as touching any thing that they shall ask, it shall be done for them of my Father which is in heaven.

For where two or three are gathered together in my name, there am I in the midst of them.

Matthew 18:19,20

6. Listen to Tapes and Read Christian Books.

We don't always have the time to sit, read, and pray. Thank God for cassette and CD players! Put in a good teaching tape and allow it to minister to you as you go about your daily work. While you are cleaning your house, put on a praise and worship tape or CD and fill your home with the presence of God. Instead of reading a popular magazine or the latest best-seller, read the story of a great man or woman of God. Read about their trials and temptations and how they overcame them to complete the plan of God. Read books on faith, healing, and deliverance, supplementing the Word of God and adding to your understanding.

7. Fellowship With Good Christian People.

Find people who uplift and encourage you. Surround yourself with those who know how to laugh and bring godly joy into your life. Fellowship with those who have the same morals, the same fervency for God, and the same purpose. Friends who fear the Lord bring a good balance into your life. If you don't have any Christian friends, ask God to bring them into your life. Through the right associations and connections, your life can be enhanced and sharpened like iron. (See Proverbs 27:17.)

VICTORY IS OURS

The enemy has deceived you once and he'll try to deceive you again. But victory is yours to have and to keep. Hold on to it with a *passion*. Do not give opportunity for the devil to control you. The Holy Spirit is your Guide and your strength. You have now been equipped with all you need, but like I said previously, it is your *choice*. Make up your mind to live an abundant life of freedom.

The thief cometh not, but for to steal, and to kill, and to destroy: I am come that they might have life, and that they might have it more abundantly.

John 10:10

CHAPTER 10
RESISTING FUTURE ATTACKS

So be subject to God. Resist the devil [stand firm against him], and he will flee from you.

James 4:7 AMP

How do we resist the enemy? Through the power of the Holy Spirit, we proclaim a strong NO! to the devil and all of hell's forces. Our own willpower is not strong enough to resist temptation — it must be through the *power* of the *Holy Spirit*.

Our *no* to the enemy must be bold and absolute. Many battles we face are unnecessary and are simply a result of not making a bold proclamation to demonic forces. It will protect the call of God on our life, our destiny, our family, and our church. There is no room for a weak *no*, or a *maybe*. There is no neutrality with God — no "summit meetings" to find a compromise.

Abhor that which is evil; cleave to that which is good.

Romans 12:9

Our carnal man does not like to hear the words *no* and *yes* — those are commitment words. People are afraid of that. The world says, "Whatever you want, it's okay. If it feels good, do it. If it is right for you, then it is right. Whatever makes you happy." That is a noabsolutes philosophy and is from the pit of hell. Resist that way of thinking at all costs.

REJECTING GUILT

People motivated by mercy can be abused more easily than others, because they feel guilty for saying *no*. However, they need to learn to say it and not feel guilty. People will run you ragged, if you let them. Demons will run you crazy, if you do not stop them.

Suppose a friend calls inviting you to a basketball game on an afternoon you had planned to spend with your family. You find it so difficult to say *no* when first asked, that you say, "Well, let me think about it."

You know you should not go, but you finally give in and go. What message did you send to your family? How were you the example of making a decision and sticking with it?

Even if you get the courage to call and cancel your plans, you feel guilty. What should have been a strong, absolute *no*, turned into a puny, miserable, guilty *no*. If you had said *no* in the first place, there would have been no guilt. All of us have fallen into this trap at one time or another.

FORGIVENESS IS LASTING

If we confess our sins, he is faithful and just to forgive us our sins, and to cleanse us from all unrighteousness.

1 John 1:9

You can be sure the enemy will try to haunt you with your past. He will say, "Yes, you have asked for the Lord's forgiveness, but how can He forgive such a big thing?"

Or he will try to trick you into thinking nothing has changed, "See, you still have those lustful thoughts. If God really forgave you, you wouldn't think this way."

Don't be deceived by the chief of all liars! Ask forgiveness, make reconciliation, and walk in love. Do not continue to ask the Lord to forgive you for something you have already laid at the cross. He removes our sin and it is as if we never committed it!

A FACADE OF MINISTRY

Don't fool yourself into believing you can withstand temptation by making it a ministry. I know one person who had a street ministry to prostitutes and homosexuals, and the next thing I knew — he was both! We are not to interview such people and get on their level in order to better relate. We are to tell them the good news, then leave! If you feel you have to befriend this type of person in order to witness to them, they most likely don't want to change. Some people simply have not reached the bottom of the barrel and are not ready for a life-changing experience.

Speak not in the ears of a fool: for he will despise the wisdom of thy words.

Proverbs 23:9

SPIRITUAL MANIPULATION

Do not allow yourself to be spiritually manipulated, as that is a form of control.

I like helping the poor, but I refuse to help lazy people. The Bible says that if you do not work, you are not to eat. (See 2 Thessalonians 3:10.) And if you do not feed your family, you are worse than an infidel. (See 1 Timothy 5:8.) Watch out for professional beggars who make the church rounds. Do not give in to their crying, whining, and begging.

Some will come to you with "words from the Lord." However, these "words" just don't set well with your spirit. Judge them according to the Word of God. Is it something that will bring glory and honor to the Lord, or is it something that will solely benefit another person? Do you feel *pressured* to do something just because someone says it is a "thus saith the Lord"? This is spiritual manipulation, often directed towards new believers, and can be very dangerous.

A certain pastor who had a tendency to be *pushy* called my office and hassled one of the men who works for me. He wanted this staff member to give him my phone number so he could discuss my holding a meeting for him.

My worker replied, "He is out on a trip right now. If you will give us your name and number, we will pass it on to him, and he will get back to you."

The pastor persisted, "Well, where is he? I will call him myself."

Our ministry policy does not permit that, and my staff knows it.

My staff member said, "We don't like to disturb him during a meeting. We'll call him and give him your name and number. Then he will call you when he can. Otherwise, you can call him when he returns."

Then this pastor yelled at my staff member. He not only yelled, but he also swore at him! The man who works for me did not yell back. He did not even tell me what had happened until some time later when we were looking over our invitations, praying about them, and working out a schedule for the future. We came to this pastor's invitation, and I asked my staff member about it. He still did not tell me what happened, but I could tell from his voice that something was not right. I know my people and I know their voices. (You need to know your family like that. You can help them in time of trouble and they can help you.)

I said, "Your voice doesn't sound right. What is the problem here?"

Then he told me what this pastor had done.

"Lose his phone number forever!" I instructed my worker.

Eventually, that pastor called again and started the whole routine, "You must come to our church. You are such a gift to the body of Christ...."

I interrupted, "Sir, would you be quiet for a moment? I want to talk to you, and I want you to know why I am doing what I am doing. I don't want any confusion here. I want you to understand me clearly.

"First of all, I am glad you called. I am glad you like my ministry and that you have read my books. That is very nice. But, I will not preach in your church. Not now, not ever — unless God specifically tells me otherwise. You have treated one of my staff members very badly. When you do something like that to one of my people, you have done it to me. And when you have done it to them or to me, you have done it to Jesus.

He began to sputter, whine, and try to explain away his actions.

But I said, "My answer to your invitation is *no*, unless God hits me on the side of the head and tells me to go to your church."

He eventually apologized, but I still did not minister in his church. I will not tolerate this type of control in my ministry.

BIBLICAL EXAMPLES OF TRAGIC CONSEQUENCES

The Bible is full of examples we can learn from of people who did not resist the enemy.

Judas Iscariot was led by his greed to betray Jesus. Afterwards, he was so grief-stricken that he hung himself from a tree. (See Matthew 27:5.)

Samson toyed with Delilah's temptations until he gave in, which led to dire consequences for him and all of Israel. (See Judges 16.)

Adam and Eve were so selfish that they listened to the voice of Satan and trusted more in him than their Creator. They, along with all of mankind, were cast out of the presence of God. (See Genesis 3.) Praise God that through His Son, Jesus Christ, we have been reconciled. (See Romans 5:17.)

King Saul turned his back on God, then lied about it to Samuel, and it cost him dearly. (See 1 Samuel 15.)

But the greatest example of a tragic consequence to sin is Lucifer.

How art thou fallen from heaven, O Lucifer, son of the morning! how art thou cut down to the ground, which didst weaken the nations!

> For thou hast said in thine heart, I will ascend into heaven, I will exalt my throne above the stars of God: I will sit also upon the mount of the congregation, in the sides of the north:
>
> I will ascend above the heights of the clouds: I will be like the most High.
>
> Yet thou shalt be brought down to hell, to the sides of the pit.
>
> Isaiah 14:12-15

God did not hesitate. He did not discuss opinions, strategies, or compromises with the devil. He did not say, "Let's have a committee meeting about this, and maybe we can share equal power." He did not ask Satan what he thought about the situation. God took immediate action, casting Satan and one-third of the angels to hell.

It does not pay to "hang out" with the wrong crowd!

Mistakes made by biblical leaders are written for our example and can save us a lot of heartache. We may not be trying to avoid a piece of fruit on a tree, but in everything we do, we have a choice to either obey or disobey. Know that there will be a price to pay for disobedience. When we are not walking under the full protection of the Lord, we are fair game for the enemy.

RELIGIOUS POLITICS

God is *powerful*, He is not *political*. Do not get bogged down with religious politics, which is *false* power. It is a major trap ministries need to avoid, because it gives people a false sense of power and influence. Let your power be from the Lord. Let Him be the One to exalt you.

If you play politics, you may think you have influence, but it will not last. The person who put you in a certain position can pull the rug right out from under you.

In religious politics, there is never a right or a wrong. There is only the strongest, or the ones with the most power and money. People who get involved in religious politics do and say things simply to please others, and usually for self-gain. That is why they do not like those who move in the prophetic giftings.

Truth is truth. When you agree with it, you are right. When you disagree, you are wrong. You cannot balance the truth. Truth already is as balanced as it is ever going to be.

When I preach the Word of God, I am right. If I preach personal convictions, I could be wrong. When I preach chapter and verse, it is right, and I do not have to apologize for it. I do not have to withdraw and consider what people are going to think of me. As long as I preach the truth, God will give me success. It is the same for anyone else. Preach the truth, and do not waver.

PROTECT YOUR FAMILY

Your home is to be your refuge — not only for you, but for every member of your family. It is to be your "safe" place. When the world around us seems like it is going down the toilet, we should be able find a safe haven within our home.

Do not let the devil get a foothold in your family! Our family is our primary ministry — our primary concern. We may be leading thousands of people to the Lord each year, but if our family is falling apart, we are not fulfilling the call of God on our life. Make this declaration the theme of your home:

As for me and my house, we will serve the Lord.
Joshua 24:15

Eli is a perfect example of a man of God who failed to train his sons in the Lord. His two sons, Hophni and Phinehas, were born into the lineage of the priesthood. They were expected to be pure and upright. However, they did not know the Lord — they were wicked. Eli did not teach them the ways of God. He let them do whatever they wanted. They used their office of priest to entice the women of Israel into illicit sex. They did not treat the Lord's offering with respect. As a result of Eli's failure to properly train his sons, they both died, he lost the priesthood for his descendants, and his descendants would bring disgrace to the family name. (See 1 Samuel 2:12-36.)

DWELLING IN HIM

As long as we are living on this planet, Satan will attempt to destroy us. Just because we have overcome one or two battles doesn't mean we are immunized against his attacks. However, we are equipped with the Word of God and His Holy Spirit to conquer anything that comes against us. We have a secret place to run to. We have confidence in Him and can trust Him for our protection.

He that dwelleth in the secret place of the most High shall abide under the shadow of the Almighty.

I will say of the Lord, He is my refuge and my fortress: my God; in him will I trust.

Surely he shall deliver thee from the snare of the fowler, and from the noisome pestilence.

He shall cover thee with his feathers, and under his wings shalt thou trust: his truth shall be thy shield and buckler.

Thou shalt not be afraid for the terror by night; nor for the arrow that flieth by day;

Nor for the pestilence that walketh in darkness; nor for the destruction that wasteth at noonday.

A thousand shall fall at thy side, and ten thousand at thy right hand; but it shall not come nigh thee.

Only with thine eyes shalt thou behold and see the reward of the wicked.

Because thou hast made the Lord, which is my refuge, even the most High, thy habitation;

There shall no evil befall thee, neither shall any plague come nigh thy dwelling.

For he shall give his angels charge over thee, to keep thee in all thy ways.

They shall bear thee up in their hands, lest thou dash thy foot against a stone.

Thou shalt tread upon the lion and adder; the young lion and the dragon shalt thou trample under feet.

Because he hath set his love upon me, therefore will I deliver him: I will set him on high, because he hath known my name.

He shall call upon me, and I will answer him: I will be with him in trouble; I will deliver him, and honour him.

With long life will I satisfy him, and show him my salvation.

Psalm 91

CHAPTER 11
GODLY CONTROL

God told Noah to build an ark. Noah built the ark. The people teased old man Noah for building such a ridiculous, useless thing. However, Noah obeyed the Lord.

After he built the ark, Noah and his family climbed into it, along with a male and female of every living creature. Oh, the reactions from his neighbors!

"What are you doing in there, Noah?"

"Hey, Noah, where is the rain?"

"It is not raining yet, you crazy nut. In fact, what is rain anyway?"

"What are you going to do with this ark-thing anyhow? Come on out, Noah. Nothing is going to happen."

But Noah stood firm, obeyed God, and was not affected by what others said about him. Was he able to do that on his own strength? Of course not! He had a personal *word* from God. (See Genesis 6:13-22.) His strength came from Jehovah.

It isn't any different with us. We have a personal *word* from God concerning our future also — it's called the Bible. The Bible, the Word of God, was written with us in mind. It's not just a history book. It was given by God Almighty to be our source of strength.

However, we have access to even more than that, and that is the Holy Spirit.

But ye shall receive power, after that the Holy Ghost is come upon you: and ye shall be witnesses unto me both in Jerusalem, and in all Judaea, and in Samaria, and unto the uttermost part of the earth.

Acts 1:8

We have a greater power within us than Noah, Abraham, and David did. I have mentioned several times that through the power of the Holy Spirit we are able to break free from controlling powers. But just exactly what does it mean to walk in that power, and is it something we can use every day?

Just as we have discussed abusive control, there is a positive side to control as well. God has ordained a good and justifiable control for our well-being. Submitting to God and being led by His Spirit will groom us and shape us into maturity.

CONTROLLED BY THE HOLY SPIRIT

The Holy Spirit is not a dictator. He does not push us, pressure us, or smother our creativity. He brings perfect balance to our lives. As beings created by God, the Holy Spirit gives us the freedom to express God through our own individual personalities.

The Holy Spirit will *convict* us of sin so we can be cleansed and go on with the plan of God. He will not *condemn* us, harass us, beat us down, or torment us, no matter how grievous our mistakes might be. He does not come to crush us, but to make us whole. His purpose is not to hold us in bondage, but to set us free.

Howbeit when he, the Spirit of truth, is come, he will guide you into all truth: for he shall not speak of himself; but whatsoever he shall hear, that shall he speak: and he will show you things to come.

John 16:13

The Holy Spirit guides us into all truth, but it is our responsibility to follow His guidance. The Holy Spirit never points to Himself, exalts Himself, or promotes Himself. He speaks only what He hears from the Father.

The Holy Spirit also helps us in our weakness. (See Romans 8:26.) He will not do the job for us, but He will help us to fulfill the plan and purpose of God for our lives. A minister friend of mine once put it this way, "The Holy Spirit will help you do a job, just as I would help you move a chair. You pick up one side of the chair, and I lift the other. That is how the Holy Spirit helps the believer."

OBEDIENCE BRINGS FAVOR

When we are living a Spirit-led life, there may be times the Lord asks us to do something that seems odd to the world. It is then we have a choice — to obey the Lord, or to submit to the world's desires. When we obey, a shield of protection is placed around us. The enemy will still try to attack, but we are sheltered from anything that comes our way. That is part of dwelling **in the secret place of the most High** (Psalm 91:1).

When God told Abraham to leave his own country, he had a decision to make — to obey God or stay where he was. (See Genesis 12.)

Abraham's relatives and friends probably thought he was crazy. There was no doubt a strong pull on him to remain in the land he knew so well with all the comforts, position, and conveniences that he had. But Abraham obeyed God.

Abraham's nephew, Lot, did not obey the Lord. When he separated from Abraham, he pitched his tent *near* Sodom. The next thing you know, he's living *in* Sodom and sitting at the city gate in the office of a city councilor. Woe unto Lot for toying with temptation.

Abraham's great-grandson, Joseph, resisted the temptations of Potiphar's wife. (See Genesis 39:6-10.) Maybe Joseph could have gotten away with having an affair, but because of his obedience and faithfulness to the Lord, many lives were saved — not just the lives of the Israelites, but the lives of many Egyptians who would have starved during the famine that came later.

Your saying *no* to demonic forces and *yes* to the obedience of Christ will also affect many lives.

Peter and John knew the value of being led by the Holy Spirit. In Acts 4, the religious leaders commanded them not to preach Christ any longer.

But the apostles said, "No. We must obey God rather than you."

And now, Lord, behold their threatenings: and grant unto thy servants, that with all boldness they may speak thy word,

By stretching forth thine hand to heal; and that signs and wonders may be done by the name of thy holy child Jesus.

And when they had prayed, the place was shaken where they were assembled together; and they were all filled with the Holy Ghost, and they spake the word of God with boldness.

Acts 4:29-31

They went out and did exactly what they had been told by man not to do and mighty miracles occurred in their ministries.

Right after this, two people lied to Peter in the presence of the Holy Spirit and dropped dead. Ananias and Sapphira said *yes* to the world and lost everything. (See Acts 5.)

From then on, Peter and John went out boldly performing miracles. They knew how to say *no* to man and *yes* to God, and signs and wonders followed.

POSITIVE CONTROL THROUGH SPIRITUAL LEADERSHIP

Positive control exercised through godly leadership helps and guides, but it does not do so for self-gain or glory. It gives an individual the freedom, within the boundaries of the Word of God, to be themselves and to express their own individual personality and creativity.

Positive control will never pressure, condemn, or smother. It will love and provide the encouragement needed to live life to the fullest for God. Positive control serves as a safety valve, a "check and balance" for our daily walk.

God has always had a leader, and spiritual leaders must exercise legitimate, godly authority. We have a responsibility to God to follow mature, seasoned leadership. We are to be submitted to such leaders, to heed their wise counsel according to the Word of God. The Holy Spirit can reveal to us the attributes to look for in those who exercise godly, positive control.

And His gifts were [varied; He Himself appointed and gave men to us,] some to be apostles (special messengers), some prophets (inspired preachers and expounders), some evangelists (preachers of the Gospel, traveling missionaries), some pastors (shepherds of His flock) and teachers.

His intention was the perfecting and the full equipping of the saints (His consecrated people), [that they should do] the work of ministering toward building up Christ's body (the church),

[That it might develop] until we all attain oneness in the faith and in the comprehension of the full and accurate knowledge of the Son of God; that [we might arrive] at really mature manhood — the completeness of personality which is nothing less than the standard height of Christ's own perfection — the measure of the stature of the fullness of the Christ, and the completeness found in Him.

So then, we may no longer be children, tossed [like ships] to and fro between chance gusts of teaching, and wavering with every changing wind of doctrine, [the prey

of] the cunning and cleverness of unscrupulous men, (gamblers engaged) in every shifting form of trickery in inventing errors to mislead.

Ephesians 4:11-14 AMP

The Lord gives certain leadership gifts to men and women to help the body of Christ come into maturity and to know Him in an intimate way. These leaders are to help equip and perfect the believers. These leadership gifts are often referred to as "the fivefold ministry."

The Greek word for **perfecting** is derived from a root word meaning to "fit, mend, prepare, restore." (See *Strong' Concordance*, #2677.)

Fit, mend, prepare, restore: These small words spell hard work and discipline. It is the job of the fivefold ministry to see to it that you and I are thoroughly endowed with faith, love, and hope, and fully equipped with the comprehension of Jesus, the works and sensitivity of the Holy Spirit, and the knowledge of every other aspect of the Word of God. They are accountable to God for their leadership over us. We, in turn, are accountable for the degree of our submission to that leadership.

Please understand that you and I are accountable to the *leadership* — the *office* and the *gifts* of the person — not the person himself. We are to follow the person as they follow the Word of God. When people in leadership positions are properly demonstrating the Scriptures, we are accountable for how we submit to the gift inside of them.

Obey your spiritual leaders and submit to them — continually recognizing their authority over you; for they are constantly keeping watch over your souls and guarding your spiritual welfare, as men who will have to render an account [of their trust]. [Do your part to] let them do this with gladness, and not with sighing and groaning, for that would not be profitable to you [either].

Hebrews 13:17 AMP

In order for a leader to "fit," "mend," "prepare," and "restore" us, there must be some degree of positive, justifiable control over our lives. Refusal to submit to such protection and wisdom would mean outright rebellion on the part of the believer. Because the body of Christ has been vague on this issue, whenever strong leadership has surfaced the people have scattered shouting, "Control! Control!"

In order to grow and become mature, we need strong leadership. If leadership is not strong, the body of Christ will not grow to full maturity. As the people of God, we need to stand behind the strong leadership that God is raising up in our midst.

There are two attitudes the church must shake: 1) compromise on the part of its leaders, and 2) despising of and rebellion against strong leadership on the part of the people.

Leadership is positive action. It is not just talking — it is actually doing something. It is moving forward with the Lord and taking the people along.

When the modern Israeli army goes into battle, its officers are sent in first, the troops then follow. This is said to be one of the reasons why the Israelis are so militarily successful. Their officers are out front, showing the troops which way to go and what to do. Other nations send their troops in first while their leaders sit well behind the lines, viewing the battle through binoculars.

That is what some church leaders are doing today — trying to lead by remaining in the background. This is partly because people do not understand good, godly, justifiable control. When leaders attempt to "fit," "mend," "prepare," or "restore" lives, the people develop a rebellious attitude and label the leadership as "controlling."

When leaders are continuously mislabeled and betrayed, they have a tendency to withdraw to protect themselves against further hurts, wounds, and slander. If you are blessed with a strong leader, follow that leader as they follow Christ.

Godly leadership will rise to the occasion and take the lead. When God speaks to them and tells their local body or nation to step out in an area of faith, they are bold to take action. Believers who are sensitive to the Spirit of God will follow and support those in leadership with all their hearts.

Strong leadership provides security for the people of God. There is hope for the world through God's strong leaders and believers! Religious, rebellious spirits do not like strong leadership! Such spirits want to dominate and control a church and its people.

Leaders must not be afraid to confront any disorderly conduct that might take place in their services. I am a strong believer in prayer and intercession, and many times some of the intercessors "get off," and begin to think they are the most spiritual people in the church. Some have even tried to use their positions to control the pastor or other leaders.

Every believer is called to the ministry of intercession. The reason some seem to be more anointed than others in the area of prayer is because they use it more! There is no scriptural reference to an "office of intercessor." An intercessor is a servant of God who is sensitive to His leading to pray His will into the earth. An intercessor paves the way for the Holy Spirit to disarrange and thwart the schemes of the enemy. Prayers of intercession make the plan of God a reality for the hour.

Intercessors must be instructed in the workings of the spirit realm and in the Word of God in order to pray accurately in the will of God. Believers must be instructed in the ways and the character of God if they are to hear Him clearly. That is not abusive control! That is the positive control of the fivefold ministry.

Pastors must not be afraid to confront intercessors that are in error. They must not be hesitant to instruct them to pray decently and in order. Leaders must not be afraid to confront and correct misdoing! That kind of godly boldness shows that they value the presence of the Holy Spirit in their midst.

If you have been confronted by a spiritual leader who has suggested that a change needs to take place in your personal life — rejoice and thank God for that individual! Yes, the searing light of the Holy Spirit hurts our flesh at times, but it is for our own good. Our spiritual growth and maturity depend on it. As the body of Christ, we are in training — so we must expect to be groomed and changed! Countless others are waiting to benefit from the training experience through which you and I will be successfully brought to full maturity.

Strong, positive control from a leader is an indication of their commitment to God. We are an army, and in order to war effectively and triumphantly, we must be united in purpose and fervency. Do not shrink back from godly leaders who have given their lives for your benefit and maturity. Be thankful for godly direction in your life. What you learn from it will be your dearest treasure on the battlefield.

THE LEADERSHIP OF MOSES

In Numbers 16, we find a very interesting situation. In the camp of the Israelites, there arose a man named Korah, a descendant of Levi, who went among the tribes complaining about the leadership of Moses. He thought Moses had taken too much power and authority upon himself as leader of God's people. In other words, Korah thought Moses was a "controller."

When Korah had secured enough backing from other disgruntled children of Israel, he and his followers approached Moses, God's chosen leader. In studying this passage, look at the type of people Korah recruited to join his cause:

> **And they rose up before Moses, with certain of the children of Israel, two hundred and fifty princes of the assembly, famous in the congregation, men of renown.**
>
> **Numbers 16:2**

Korah did not have God behind him, so he had to recruit the most famous men among the tribes of Israel in an attempt to give himself validity. When these dissenters — including many of the other Levites who served in the temple worship — had assembled together, they approached Moses and Aaron. There Korah presented his accusation against these men of God:

> **They came as a group to oppose Moses and Aaron and said to them, "You have gone too far! The whole community is holy, every one of them, and the Lord is with them. Why then do you set yourselves above the Lord's assembly?"**
>
> **Numbers 16:3 NIV**

Korah could not understand why Moses was in the place of leadership. These Israelites did not recognize the divine control that had been given to Moses and Aaron by God Himself. Instead they were driven by jealousy, motivated by their desire for power, and blinded to the truth by religion and rebellion.

Divine leadership involves a heavy price. If it were not for the grace of God, the weight of it, at times, would be almost unbearable. The main price that must be paid by a leader concerns the daily life they must lead before the people. The leader's life is often scrutinized and closely monitored.

Divine leaders must pursue the way of righteousness and holiness. They must have a strong desire for God and hate evil with all their heart. Compromise will weaken an individual's ability to take a strong stand against Satan.

When we are strong and refuse to bow to evil, there will be those who will try to find something wrong with us in order to destroy our character, undermine our stand, and overcome our strength. But divine leaders must be faithful, no matter what comes against them. God will move the foundations of the earth for the faithful.

Divine leaders must be spiritually discerning. They will not change their stand just because they are under attack from the enemy. They will continue to obey God in the midst of conflict and adversity.

After Moses had heard the accusation levied against him and Aaron by Korah and his followers, he fell on his face before the Lord. Then he rose up to speak to Korah and the sons of Levi who were with him:

Then he said to Korah and all his followers: "In the morning the Lord will show who belongs to him and who is holy, and he will have that person come near him. The man he chooses he will cause to come near him.

"Isn't it enough for you that the God of Israel has separated you from the rest of the Israelite community and brought you near himself to do the work at the Lord's tabernacle and to stand before the community and minister to them?

"He has brought you and all your fellow Levites near himself, but now you are trying to get the priesthood too."
Numbers 16:5,9,10

The Lord had already chosen Korah to stand in His house and minister to Him before the people, but that was a minor thing to Korah. He wasn't satisfied with the position God had called him to. Moses prophesied that the Lord would show everyone who His chosen leader was.

Moses was instructed by God to have the people choose the side they were on: Korah's or Moses'. After the children of Israel had run to whichever side they had chosen, Moses warned the people that if the Lord was on his side, the earth would open up and swallow the rebellious Korah and his group, because they had provoked the Lord their God. The Bible records that as soon as Moses had finished speaking, the earth did open up and swallow Korah, his people, and all his goods. God then sent a fire to consume all the murmurers who had gathered with Korah. (See Numbers 16:30-35.)

God will never forsake the godly leaders He has ordained, no matter who or what should rise up against them. Moses continually showed his heart for the people. He confronted the people with bold leadership in order to turn them back to the Lord.

THE LEADERSHIP OF PAUL

For though ye have ten thousand instructors in Christ, yet have ye not many fathers: for in Christ Jesus I have begotten you through the gospel.

Wherefore I beseech you, be ye followers of me.

I Corinthians 4:15,16

Look at the security Paul enjoyed in his position as a leader! He wanted the people to follow his example and lifestyle.

Would you say that Paul practiced abusive control? Of course not! Yet I dare say that if a leader today should make such a bold statement as this one, many would have him labeled before the sun came up!

Brethren, be followers together of me, and mark them which walk so as ye have us for an ensample.

Philippians 3:17

Not only did Paul tell the Philippian believers to follow his lifestyle, he also said that they should watch those who followed him, for they were good examples of Christianity. That is secure leadership!

As a leader chosen and anointed by God, Paul took his responsibility seriously. He watched carefully over the flock of believers under his authority.

For I am jealous over you with godly jealousy: for I have espoused you to one husband, that I may present you as a chaste virgin to Christ.

2 Corinthians 11:2

Paul had a godly jealousy over those he had brought to Jesus. He was constantly on guard against anyone or anything that might come to steal the people of God away from their first love — Jesus Christ. He fought against the sin that might blemish the church. He did not hesitate to confront, because of the love he had for Jesus. He wanted all believers to come into the full maturity that the resurrection had provided for them. He took the risk of being hated, persecuted, and killed so that lives could be saved. That is not abusive control — that is *positive, justifiable, godly leadership!*

Am I now trying to win the approval of men, or of God? Or am I trying to please men? If I were still trying to please men, I would not be a servant of Christ.

Galatians 1:10 NIV

Paul never desired or sought to be exalted by men. He was a true servant of God.

The whole key to positive, biblical control is the fact that no matter how many decisions we make, how many conversions we produce, how many people are healed or delivered by our message, how many foes we conquer — our primary concern is that Jesus Christ be seen first and foremost in every situation we face.

WE ARE EQUIPPED

Paul was probably one of the most influential men in the New Testament. He had a greater impact on furthering the Gospel message than any other man except Jesus. He was very instrumental in the development of the New Testament Church — starting churches, evangelizing multitudes, and discipling others. His attitude towards the trials and persecution he suffered is an example of true Christianity — one we should all follow. Even in his suffering, God was glorified.

For our light affliction, which is but for a moment, worketh for us a far more exceeding and eternal weight of glory.

2 Corinthians 4:17

Sound impossible? The good news is that it *is* possible! Paul, along with the other New Testament apostles and evangelists, were able to do all that they did through the power of the Holy Spirit.

For with God nothing shall be impossible.

Luke 1:37

God will not ask us to do something and not provide the means to accomplish it. You don't ask your son to mow the lawn and not teach him how to use the lawn mower. But if your son refuses to use the lawn mower, he will find it very difficult to properly and successfully mow the lawn. God does not ask us to walk and live in the Spirit without providing the Holy Spirit. But if we refuse the Holy Spirit's guidance and direction, we will find it very difficult to live the abundant life promised to us.

Receive your freedom from demonic, abusive controlling powers. Walk in the power of the Holy Spirit. Experience life the way God intended you to — free!

CONCLUSION

By applying the principles in this book to your life, you can be set free and live a free life in Jesus Christ. When you are free from demonic and abusive controlling powers and allow the Holy Spirit to have control, you can walk in forgiveness, wisdom, and strength. When controlling powers come your way again, you will recognize them for what they are, be able to stand against them, and overcome them.

Casting down imaginations, and every high thing that exalteth itself against the knowledge of God, and bringing into captivity every thought to the obedience of Christ.
2 Corinthians 10:5

Do not live in fear that what you have been set free from will happen again. Take captive any negative words that have been spoken over you and claim the promises of God for your life. Leave your past experiences in the past, including hurts and wounds inflicted by loved ones. God has a great future planned for you!

Let the Word of God be your standard. Judge everything by the Word — dividing the truth from the lies and accurately discerning the difference between hindrances and blessings. There is no attack planned against you that you cannot win through the power of the Holy Spirit.

No weapon that is formed against thee shall prosper; and every tongue that shall rise against thee in judgment thou shalt condemn. This is the heritage of the servants of the Lord, and their righteousness is of me, saith the Lord.
Isaiah 54:17

FIVE *NO* FACTS

1. *No* is one of the words people most wish they had said in past situations.

A young lady who graduated from high school with me is an example. By the time she was in her early twenties, she was divorced and a single mother — all because she did not say *no* one night to her boyfriend.

People are pastoring wrong churches because they did not say *no*.

Some Christians have lost their rewards or crowns in heaven because they did not say *no* at the right time.

2. *No* originated in heaven with God.

No and *yes* are appropriate responses to right and wrong. God originated these responses.

3. *No* protects you and stops the devil.

No would have protected the young lady I mentioned above and her entire life would have been different.

4. *No* is a part of the teachings of the Bible.

We have already discussed a number of people from the Bible who said *no* when they should have said *yes*, or vice versa. The consequences of their actions are plainly written out for all who will read them to profit by.

5. *No* can be said by anyone.

You do not have to be fifty years old in the Lord before you can say *no*. You can be five seconds old in Jesus and say no. The Holy Spirit has given us the power to say no.

ONE *YES* FACT

1. *Yes* to Jesus says it all.

MY PRAYER FOR YOU

Father, I thank You for this message on control. I thank You for the understanding that You are giving us and the wisdom to discern accurately the difference between hindrances and blessings in our lives. We give You the glory for it.

I thank You, Father, that You want to see people set free from the power of abusive control. I send the Word of God to them now, and I break the power of controlling spirits over them: Satan, let the people go free, in Jesus' name!

I break the power of fear. I tear down negative words that have been spoken over people, and I call for clarity and direction to come to them so they can fulfill Your plan for their lives.

I thank You, Lord, that You are giving them revelation concerning their circumstances, so they can know what to do to be set free.

Father, I thank You that not one person feels that I am against them.

Thank You, Father, for the strong leadership You are causing to come forth now through the body of Christ. We ask You for the boldness to be witnesses of the Gospel in greater power and manifestation. Your purposes shall be fulfilled in the earth!

Let the Word begin to divide the truth from the lies and bring forth freedom in people's lives, so their homes may be filled with Your presence, power, and joy.

In Jesus' name, we thank You for these things and expect to receive them.

Amen.

ABOUT THE AUTHOR

Roberts Liardon is President of Roberts Liardon Ministries and Founder and Senior Pastor of Embassy Christian Center in Irvine, California. He is also Founder of Spirit Life Bible College and Life Ministerial Association in Irvine.

Roberts Liardon received his call to ministry as an eight-year-old boy. Since then, he has diligently endeavored to follow that call through preaching and teaching God's Word. He has preached in over eighty nations with extensive ministry in Europe, Asia, and Africa.

As a best-selling author, Roberts has expanded his ministry onto the printed page. His books have been translated into over twenty-seven languages and have been circulated throughout the world. Roberts' books reflect his belief that the Church can fulfill its call and bring revival to the nations by combining God's Word with the moving of His Spirit.

As a historian, Roberts holds a wealth of knowledge regarding the great leaders of three Christian movements — Pentecostal, Divine Healing, and Charismatic. He embarked on his in-depth studies as a fourteen-year-old and continued those studies into adulthood. Roberts has established ongoing research through the founding of Reformers and Revivalist Historial Museum in California.

BOOKS BY ROBERTS LIARDON

Breaking Controlling Powers

Smith Wigglesworth Speaks to Students of the Bible

Sharpen Your Discernment

Smith Wigglesworth:
The Complete Collection of His Life Teachings

God's Generals

God's Generals Workbook

A Call to Action

Cry of the Spirit:
Unpublished Sermons by Smith Wigglesworth

Forget Not His Benefits

Haunted Houses, Ghosts & Demons

Holding to the Word of the Lord

I Saw Heaven

Kathryn Kuhlman:
A Spiritual Biography of God's Miracle-Working Power

Religious Politics

Run to the Battle

School of the Spirit

Spiritual Timing

The Invading Force

The Price of Spiritual Power

The Quest for Spiritual Hunger

Also Available:

God's Generals Video Collection

(12 Video Tapes)

A SPECIAL NOTE FROM ROBERTS LIARDON

We are building the God's Generals Library/Museum in an effort to preserve Christian Pentecostal history. We are accepting any memorabilia, such as (but not limited to) magazines, pamphlets, audio tapes, video tapes, books, letters, scrapbooks, ledgers, photographs, newspapers, or personal artifacts. Donations such as personal Bibles and clothing, even the very instruments used in the meetings of the Pentecostal generals, are accepted and greatly appreciated. Many of the items are reproduced onto microfilm so that generations to come can experience their Christian heritage.

If you have anything you would like to donate to Christian history, no matter how large or how small, or if you know of someone who would like to contribute, please call our Research Department at 949-833-3555, or write to me at the following address:

Roberts Liardon
Attn: Research Department
P. O. Box 30710
Laguna Hills, California 92654-0710

Thank you for sharing your portion of history with the world and with the generations to come. Only heaven can reveal the lives you will have touched by your thoughtful generosity.

Seven reasons you should attend Spirit Life Bible College

1. SLBC is a **spiritual school** with an academic support; not an academic school with a spiritual touch.

2. SLBC teachers are **successful ministers** in their own right. Pastor Roberts Liardon will not allow failure to be imparted into his students.

3. SLBC is a member of **Oral Roberts University Educational Fellowship** and will be fully **accredited** with the International Christian Accrediting Association July '98.

4. SLBC hosts monthly seminars with some of the **world's greatest** ministers who add another element, anointing and impartation to the students' lives.

5. Roberts Liardon understands your commitment to come to SLBC and commits himself to students by **ministering weekly** in classroom settings.

6. SLBC provides **hands-on** ministerial training.

7. SLBC provides ministry opportunity through its **post-graduate placement program**.

-------------------- CLIP ALONG LINE & MAIL TO ROBERTS LIARDON MINISTRIES. --------------------

Spirit Life Partner

Wouldn't It Be Great...

- If you could feed over 1,000 hungry people every week?
- If you could travel 250,000 air miles, boldly preaching the Word of God in 90 nations?
- If you could strengthen and train the next generation of God's leaders?
- If you could translate 23 books and distribute them into 37 countries?

Project Joseph Food Outreach.

...Now You Can!

Maybe you can't go, but by supporting this ministry every month, your gift can help to communicate the Gospel around the world.

-------------------- CLIP ALONG LINE & MAIL TO ROBERTS LIARDON MINISTRIES. --------------------

☐ **YES!!** Pastor Roberts, I want to support your work in the kingdom of God by becoming a **SPIRIT LIFE PARTNER.** Please find enclosed my first monthly gift.

Name_____

Address_____

City_____ State_____ Zip_____

Phone (_____)_____

SPIRIT LIFE PARTNER AMOUNT: $_____

☐ Check / Money Order ☐ VISA ☐ American Express ☐ Discover ☐ MasterCard

☐☐☐☐ ☐☐☐☐ ☐☐☐☐ ☐☐☐☐

Name On Card_____ Exp. Date____/___/

Signature_____ Date ____/___/

Roberts Liardon Ministries

P.O. Box 30710 ♦ Laguna Hills, CA 92654 ♦ (949) 833-3555 ♦ Fax (949) 833.9555 ♦ www.robertsliardon.org

ROBERTS LIARDON MINISTRIES INTERNATIONAL OFFICES:

EUROPE
Roberts Liardon Ministries
P. O. Box 2043
Hove, Brighton
East Sussex, BN3 6JU England
Phone and Fax: 44 1273 777427

SOUTH AFRICA
Roberts Liardon Ministries
P. O. Box 3155
Kimberley 8300, South Africa
Phone and Fax: 27 531 82 1207

AUSTRALIA
Roberts Liardon Ministries
P. O. Box 439
Buderim QLD 4556
Australia
Phone: 011 61 754 422108

USA
Roberts Liardon Ministries
P. O. Box 30710
Laguna Hills, California 92654
Phone: (949) 833-3555
Fax: (949) 833-9555
email: www.robertsliardon.org

Additional copies of this book and other book titles from
ALBURY PUBLISHING
are available at your local bookstore.

Albury Publishing
P. O. Box 470406
Tulsa, Oklahoma 74147-0406

In Canada books are available from:
Word Alive
P. O. Box 670
Niverville, Manitoba
CANADA R0A 1E0